/GM Opportunities Series

OPPORTUNITIES IN **AUTOMOTIVE SERVICE CAREERS**

Robert M. Weber

Revised by
Philip A. Perry

Foreword by
Ronald H. Weiner
President
National Institute for Automotive Service Excellence

VGM Career Books

*Chicago   New York   San Francisco   Lisbon   London   Madrid   Mexico City
Milan   New Delhi   San Juan   Seoul   Singapore   Sydney   Toronto*

Library of Congress Cataloging-in-Publication Data

Weber, Robert M.
 Opportunities in automotive service careers / Robert M. Weber; revised by Philip A. Perry; foreword by Ronald Weiner.—Rev. ed.
p.c.—(VGM opportunities series)
ISBN 0-07-138203-8 (hardcover) – ISBN 0-07-138195-3 (paperback)
1. Automobiles—Maintenance and repair—Vocational guidance. I. Title. II. Series

TL152.W37 2001
629.28'72'023—dc21

2001026428

VGM Career Books

A Division of The **McGraw·Hill** *Companies*

1 2 3 4 5 6 7 8 9 0   LBM/LBM   0 9 8 7 6 5 4 3 2 1

ISBN 0-07-138203-8 (hardcover)
    0-07-138195-3 (paperback)

This book was set in Times by Publication Services, Inc.
Printed and bound by Lake Book Manufacturing

Cover photograph copyright © PhotoDisc

McGraw-Hill books are available at special quantity discounts to use as premiums and sales promotions, or for use in corporate training programs. For more information, please write to the Director of Special Sales, Professional Publishing, McGraw-Hill, Two Penn Plaza, New York, NY 10121-2298. Or contact your local bookstore.

This book is printed on acid-free paper.

To my wife Judy . . .
Because cars need drivers—and so do some writers.

CONTENTS

ABOUT THE AUTHOR

Robert M. Weber is a nationally syndicated auto service columnist, writing about car repair. He was the director of regulatory affairs at the National Institute for Automotive Service Excellence (ASE) and formerly editor of *Super Automotive Service* magazine, a monthly trade journal circulated to businesses such as full-service service stations, independent repair shops, tire stores, oil jobbers, and mass merchandisers.

Prior to joining the staff of *Super Automotive Service,* he was the operations manager for a chain of midwestern exhaust and auto repair shops. He is a certified master automotive technician by the National Institute for Automotive Service Excellence (ASE) and an affiliate member of the Society of Automotive Engineers (SAE).

His automotive career began in 1964 when he worked as a service station attendant while in high school, and he continued as a part-time mechanic while earning a degree in speech communications from Geneva College in Pennsylvania.

This book has been revised by Philip A. Perry, a freelance writer living in Evanston, IL.

FOREWORD

Back in the early 1900s, Grandpa and Grandma were relaxing on the front porch with an iced tea when the very first automobile they ever saw went by. It was a loud clanging thing that smoked and sputtered and had two dim lantern headlights. Grandma said, "What in the world is that thing?" "I don't know," replied Grandpa, "but let me get my gun." Grandpa ran into the house, grabbed his gun, and hurried back to the porch. He took aim and fired at the car, causing the driver to jump out and run away in terror. "Did you kill it?" Grandma asked him. "No, but I sure made that monster turn the man loose!"

This old joke symbolizes the mixed emotions we have about automobiles. As a nation, we love the convenience and freedom of personal transportation, but we are less thrilled about traffic jams, the price of gasoline, and car maintenance. Today, automobiles are an essential part of our lives, and the automotive industry is an essential part of our economy.

If you are exploring career options, I urge you to consider the automotive industry. It's a wide field with a range of challenging opportunities. When one hears mention of a career in the automotive industry, one generally thinks of automotive mechanics or technicians; however, that essential function is only a part of a much larger industry. In addition to technicians, there are salespeople, engineers, warehouse managers, writers, editors, instructors, business executives, and many others working in this important field.

This career book concentrates on the service and repair aspect of our industry and rightfully so, since it is the technicians who keep our cars, trucks, and sport utility vehicles running. With today's high-tech cars, auto mechanics, who are also called "auto technicians," have never been more valuable or in greater demand. The old grease-monkey stereotypes are history; today, people recognize technicians as skilled, respected professionals. For example, working technicians can prove their skills on the job while earning professional certification through the National Institute for Automotive Service Excellence (ASE), much in the same way that doctors, lawyers, plumbers, and electricians are certified.

Most car owners have a difficult time making sense of the components found under the hoods of their automobiles, and that's why skilled mechanics always will be in demand. Because of improving technology, the skills required to excel in this field are becoming more complex. Auto technicians should have a thorough educational background in math, science, and especially computers, since almost all of the average automobile's functions are controlled and maintained by computers. In addition, courses in English will be helpful, because strong communication skills are essential in any business environment. For the best and the brightest students, those with an interest in continued learning and a strong work ethic, a career in this exciting and necessary industry is well worth considering. Good luck!

Ronald H. Weiner
President
National Institute for Automotive Service Excellence

PREFACE

We need sixty to eighty thousand more auto technicians than we have today. What's more, we need for them to be skilled technicians. The growing need for automotive technicians is a major concern nationwide. Among all jobs that have been considered "careers without college," auto technician ranks as one of the best. It can pay off right out of high school. Yet it's a job that requires intelligence and advanced skills. To reach the top of the profession today, it is necessary to have training beyond high school. The major auto manufacturers all have launched outreach programs to attract high school students early on and show them the possibilities and challenges of an automotive service career. They all emphasize that extra training will be amply rewarded. If you can step up to the challenge of an accredited auto technology training course at a local college along with, possibly, an apprenticeship at a manufacturer's dealership or an independent repair shop, you will find your skills in great demand in the job market after you graduate. This revised edition emphasizes and reinforces Robert M. Weber's main points made in the first edition: good initial training, knowledge of tools and equipment, and certification through recognized industry sources, along with continuing education. The reviser gratefully acknowledges the assistance of many sources in the automotive industry, including the Institute for Auto Service Excellence, the Automobile Service Association, I–CAR, the Automotive Aftermarket Industry Association, and others. In addition, the Bureau of Labor Statistics was helpful in furnishing up-to-date data on employment and earnings.

INTRODUCTION

No one really knows when the wheel was invented, but ever since, people have been rolling things from one place to another.

In the beginning, people themselves were their only means of transportation. The use of domesticated animals followed. It wasn't until the industrial age that other means of propulsion—inanimate sources—were harnessed. Steam power was first, and electricity was at one time believed to be the ultimate answer. "In fifteen years, more electricity will be sold for electric vehicles than for light," said Thomas Edison in 1910. Although we may see a return to the electric car, it had its heyday at the turn of the century, when ten thousand were built. Ironically, it was the electric starter, invented at the same time, that made the gasoline car more practical. Since that time, greater and greater numbers of automobiles have become a part of American life.

Machines break down and wear out. The idea that one is a mechanic usually begins with having to fix one's own car. Unless you have plenty of money, your car is usually a cheap, used one. Soon things begin to wear out, and the car breaks down. To save money, you begin making those minor repairs. You're fixing cars. For some reason, it is a satisfying experience. You buy a few more tools to make the job easier. You've got grease under your fingernails—oil in your blood. Suddenly, you're hooked.

Before long, some of your friends are asking you to help them fix their cars, and you're calling yourself a mechanic. And you're not alone. Many of your peers are doing the same thing. But which of you will become the professional? *Only* those who will learn and understand the principles involved and those who get the training. The real mechanics will be those who devote themselves to being the best in their fields. It takes time, energy, drive, desire, and an inquisitive mind. Like a doctor, lawyer, or business executive, the professional automotive service technician is a trained, disciplined worker who must continue to learn all through his or her career.

There are more than 500 million passenger cars in the world. Of that total, 25 percent, or more than 125 million cars are in the United States. Canada has 14 million cars and 4 million trucks. The population of trucks and buses in the world adds another 147 million commercial vehicles, with 76 million trucks and buses in the United States alone. At one time or another, each and every one of these vehicles will need service. It may be as simple as an oil change or as complicated as a transmission rebuild. In fact, the Automotive Aftermarket Industry Association (AAIA) estimated that about 80 percent of the vehicles on the road needed some kind of service.

Mechanics are the people who keep all those vehicles running. Unfortunately, the term *mechanic* has some negative connotations. Too many people have the impression that mechanics are like those often portrayed on television as inarticulate, simple, bumbling idiots. The automotive technician (mechanic) is no less a professional than the computer repair technician or television repair technician. In this book, the terms *mechanic* and *technician* will be used interchangeably. It is a profession of which one may be proud. Without the professional automotive service technician, this country's transportation would come to a screeching halt.

According to the U.S. Department of Labor, in 1997 there were 631,000 automotive service jobs that accounted for more than $14.8 billion in wages. A full one out of five people in America works in the transportation industry in one kind of job or another, and 12 percent of personal expenditures in America are for maintenance and operation of motor vehicles.

There is currently a real need for qualified automotive technicians, and the outlook is even brighter for the future. There always will be a job for the skilled, quality technician, but it takes work to become one. If you think you've got the right qualifications, read on.

CHAPTER 1

FROM WHEELS TO AUTOMOBILES

For most of us, it is hard to imagine a time when there was no automobile. However, as far as history is concerned, the motorcar is an extremely recent development. The first self-propelled road vehicle emerged in about 1800, but it was a steam vehicle, not an internal combustion, engine-driven machine. It wasn't until about 1900 that the gasoline-powered car came into existence. Even then it was more a novelty than a viable means of transportation.

DREAMER OF DREAMS

Leonardo da Vinci, back in the 1500s, was probably the first dreamer to envision a self-propelled vehicle. There was no way his ideas could be put to use, because at the time there was no such thing as a dependable engine. In the eighteenth century, a French artillery officer, Nicholas Joseph Cugnot, designed and built a three-wheeled carriage powered by a steam engine.

EUROPE LEADS THE WAY

During the first half of the nineteenth century, there was a great deal of experimentation in Great Britain. Most of the work revolved around steam buses.

It was generally agreed at the time that steam was the answer, but in France and America work was underway to develop an internal combustion engine. The first was a two-cycle engine patented in Paris by the Belgian Étienne Lenoir. Meanwhile in America, George B. Brayton designed a two-cycle engine, which he displayed at the Philadelphia Continental Exposition in 1876. The first four-cycle engine was developed by a German, Nicholas Otto, in 1878. These early engines weren't designed for cars, but for industrial application. The distinction of inventing the first motorcar goes to Siegfried Markus of Vienna. Yet, Markus did not have an operational car until about the mid-1880s.

Back in the United States, a patent attorney named George B. Selden from Rochester, New York, felt that Brayton's engine could be put to use in a road vehicle. In 1879 Selden filed an application for a United States patent on the road engine—a motor that used liquid hydrocarbon fuel (gasoline), a mechanism to uncouple the engine from the drive wheels (the first clutch), and a steering device. But he never built a vehicle with any of these elements, and his patents eventually created some controversy in the American auto industry.

About the same time, another method of propulsion came into being—the electric motor. Suddenly, there were some options. But what good are power plants if there aren't any vehicles to put them in? Enter the bicycle industry.

FROM BIKES TO CARS

In England in 1885, J. K. Starley invented the safety bicycle, which was the first of the low-wheeled type we still enjoy today. It replaced the high-wheeled velocipede, which had one big wheel in the front and took quite some strength to pedal. Starley's bike, with its low wheels, was safer and had one more important advantage—it was driven by a chain and had gearing. The safety bicycle could be used easily by women and children. The sudden popularity of bicycles made it immediately apparent that American roads were insufficient. Bicyclists in America called for something to be done, and Congress instituted the Bureau of Road Inquiry under the Department of Agriculture to study the situation. Congress appropriated $1,000 for the job. Coincidentally, the year was 1893—the same year the Duryea car made its debut.

Bicycle manufacturers were responsible for much more. They invented steel-tube framing that combined strength with light weight. They were responsible for the chain drive, as well as ball and roller bearings. During the height of the bicycle craze, the manufacturers invented the differential gearing arrangement for use on multiple-geared bikes. The importance of the bicycle industry becomes obvious if you take a look at the bicycle companies that later crossed the bridge to the auto. In Germany there was Opel; in England, Morris; and in the United States, Duryea, Pope, Winton, and Willys.

Perhaps one of the most significant inventions leading to the motorcar was the pneumatic tire perfected by John B. Dunlop of Ireland in 1888. Without the development of good roads and the pneumatic tire, there probably would not have been much incentive for highway travel, since rail transportation was much easier and speedier.

THE SECOND GENERATION

The direct ancestors of today's automobile had their beginnings at the hands of two Germans, Karl Benz and Gottlieb Daimler, who both made internal-combustion engines. Both men made single-cylinder engines. Daimler's, however, was a high-speed engine that relied on something called a hot tube, while Benz was using a spark ignition much like today's engines. Both first put their engines to use in some sort of bicycle.

Within ten years, cars were being built. In France, Armand Peugeot was putting Daimler engines in cars for the firm of Panhard and Levassor. At the same time, William Steinway was trying to interest the American people in the German engine, but without success.

Europe was buzzing with self-propelled vehicles powered with everything from gasoline to steam to electricity. There were road races and exhibitions everywhere. Levassor won a race in Paris in 1894 and the next year drove a Panhard from Paris to Bordeaux, covering 1,200 kilometers in the remarkable time of forty-eight hours. His average speed was fifteen miles per hour.

These cars were hand built. There was no such thing as a repair shop. Cars were expensive to build and operate, and they were nothing more than a curiosity for the rich to play with. But by the turn of the century, high society began to accept the motor vehicle for use as a limousine, and ladies as well as men were driving electric vehicles.

THE ERA OF AMERICAN AUTOS

The era of the automobile in the United States really began in September 1893, when a couple of bicycle mechanics drove a one-cylinder machine through the streets of Springfield, Massachusetts. Frank and Charles Duryea had read a description of Benz's car in *Scientific American* and decided to build their own.

The *Chicago Times-Herald* helped the development of the automobile in another way: it sponsored races. In November 1895 the Duryea brothers entered a two-cylinder car, and they won. Who were the mechanics? The Duryeas had to do all the repairs themselves. The mechanics were the people who built the cars.

COMMERCIAL PRODUCTION

At about the same time, Hiram Percy Maxim, a graduate of the Massachusetts Institute of Technology, went to work for the American Projectile Company. He got together a used tricycle, some empty shell casings, and a couple of cups of gasoline. He experimented to see what would happen when gas was ignited in a cylinder. Fortunately, he didn't kill himself. He eventually built an engine that he put on his used tricycle, and it worked—sort of. But what is important is that he attracted the attention of the Pope Manufacturing Company. Pope was the world's largest maker of bicycles, and the company offered Maxim a job as chief engineer of motor carriages. This marked the beginning of the first commercial effort at motor vehicle production in America. However, Albert Pope, the owner, had Maxim building electric cars, since Pope believed that people would be afraid to sit over an explosion. The engines were usually placed under the seats. Within a couple of years, the Pope Company had built about five hundred electric vehicles and forty gasoline ones. The Popes had been making bicycles sold under the name Columbia, so they kept the name for their cars. The cars were called the Columbia Mark III Electric Phaetons.

In September 1895 the first American company was organized to produce gasoline cars. Organized by Frank and Charles Duryea, it was appropriately called the Duryea Motor Wagon Company.

In June 1896 Henry Ford drove his quadracycle down the streets of Detroit. Although Ford did not build the first American automobile, he did sell his quadracycle for $200 dollars to Charles Ainsley of Detroit. Ford was probably the first used car salesman. At the same time, the French word *automobile* was beginning to appear in print in American publications.

DETROIT: MOTOR CITY

Two other companies were organized in 1897. The first auto company in Michigan was organized on August 21, by Ransom E. Olds. He called his firm the Olds Motor Vehicle Company, but it failed, so he reorganized it two years later as the Olds Motor Works. He developed his curved dash Run-about in 1901 and sold it for $650, making it the first low-priced car. Unfortunately, fire destroyed his Detroit plant that year, so he moved the operation to Lansing, only to sell it two years later. It ultimately became the Oldsmobile division of General Motors.

As a result of the fire, and in order to get back into business, Olds had to use his one and only car as a sample for building others. He was forced to contract for parts and subassemblies from small shops in the Detroit area. Most of these subcontractors eventually decided to get into auto making themselves, and consequently Detroit became the "Motor City."

A BOOMING INDUSTRY

By 1899 the American auto industry was blossoming. The American Motor Company in New York opened a garage and advertised that it had "competent mechanics always on hand to make repairs when necessary." Meanwhile in Boston, the Back Bay Cycle and Motor Company opened a shop for "renting, sales, storage, and repair of motor vehicles."

In 1900 many of the United States manufacturers at last moved the engine from under the driver's seat to under a hood. The gasoline car finally beat a steam car in a free-for-all race held at the Washington Park horse-racing track outside of Chicago. Something else happened that was to ultimately put gasoline engines ahead of steam and electric. The tremendous gusher called "Spindletop" near Beaumont, Texas, came in on January 10, 1901. The price of crude went down to five cents a barrel. The irony of this is that gasoline was formerly considered a waste by-product that was burned off in the production of lubricants. With the advent of the gasoline engine, it was suddenly in demand, and because of its ready availability, it was cost-effective to use. Besides, steam engines needed a trained technician to control the burners and valves on board. The gasoline engine could operate by itself, so the driver did not need a helper.

America had entered the automotive age in a big way—soon to be bigger than any country in the world. Who was responsible for bringing it along? The technician, whose know-how and eagerness to learn made the American mechanic an essential ingredient in the development of the industry.

CHAPTER 2

NEW HORIZONS

For the person who brings the right talents to automotive repair, the field is wide open. More and more people are needed to keep America rolling.

The automotive industry is not limited to cars. Almost anything that has an engine and moves is part of the industry. Technicians are needed to keep all of the equipment running, and that includes about 193 million cars, trucks, and buses. That's not counting the many more millions of off-highway vehicles like farm tractors, road-building equipment, and other mechanized equipment—forklifts, bulldozers, motorcycles, military machines, and many, many more.

Most of the companies performing automotive service are small. They are part of the backbone businesses that make the United States the great nation of free enterprise that it is.

Transportation is an essential part of this country's basic health and well-being, but we tend to forget how vital it is to all of us. Every year in America, we roll up almost two trillion miles. Motor vehicles carry people, freight, food, and fire and construction equipment from one place to another. We seldom stop even to think about it, because it is so woven into the fabric of American life. We consider even less often the huge industry that keeps everything moving.

Let something break down, however, and we expect almost immediate repairs. One of the most devastating phrases a motorist can hear is "you'll have to leave it overnight." The automotive industry is responsible for getting the parts and tools to the right place at the right time, with the right people to make the right repairs.

We demand quick and proper repairs for our vehicles and we deserve as much when we part with our money. The person doing the job must be well trained, have the right tools and equipment, and be conscientious enough to do the job right the first time. An auto repair mechanic, or technician, is an important and valuable commodity and certainly deserves our respect.

SHADE TREE MECHANIC

There was a time when a person did not need formal training in order to fix automobiles. In fact, it's a major problem that any person who buys a handful of wrenches may use the label of "mechanic."

Times, and cars, have changed. There are, of course, a few who think it is still possible to get into the field of automobile repair by the trial-and-error method. Some of these people may even land jobs. It is not likely, however, that a person can hold a position of respect, or can advance, without adequate formal training. The self-trained mechanic usually becomes known as a "parts changer"—that is, the person who cannot diagnose problems. Maybe the person has an aptitude for things mechanical and perhaps is also good with his or her hands. But an untrained person will never become a reliable and disciplined automotive technician.

THE PROFESSIONAL TECHNICIAN

The true professional automotive technician must learn and apply his or her trade in a formal manner. That means learning the right way—not by trial and error. Nothing can replace formal training.

Where does the person interested in a career in the automotive repair industry receive training? There are several avenues. The person may begin in high school by taking advantage of the automotive training programs offered in most schools. A fortunate person may train under the direction of a master technician, and as an apprentice will learn while doing. However, apprenticeship opportunities are not as widely available as they once were. Instead, many technicians are going on from high school to a certificate program or a two-year degree. Fortunately, numerous vocational training schools and colleges offer good automotive courses. The automobile manufacturers and oil companies also conduct training programs.

The field of automobile repair has grown exceedingly fast in the past few years. There is even debate as to whether the general mechanic is a thing of the past. The general mechanic is one who can fix and diagnose all systems from ignition to brakes to suspension and steering to transmissions and more. With the growing sophistication of the automobile, it is almost impossible to know all the systems intimately and understand them all well enough to repair them. Many technicians now specialize.

SPECIALISTS AND THE HOLISTIC APPROACH

The trend is toward the specialist in the automotive arena. Just a quick look in the telephone directory reveals that there are specialists in suspension, brakes, transmissions, exhaust, and diesels for both autos and trucks, as well as tune-up specialists, electrical specialists, body repairers and painters, and even management.

As much as it seems that specialization is the wave of the future, it is important for any technician to take a holistic approach to automotive repair. Let's examine a hypothetical case.

A customer complains of transmission problems. The shifting does not occur at the proper time or speed. If the transmission specialist test-drives the vehicle, he or she may agree that indeed the problem is in the transmission. But the automatic transmission often relies on engine vacuum and throttle pressure—or even computers—to determine the correct shift point. So if the transmission expert is unaware of the function of the engine, the problem may be incorrectly diagnosed as strictly transmission-related. The actual reason may be a vacuum-related problem. A leak in the engine's intake manifold will result in insufficient vacuum for the transmission modulator to function. A transmission rebuild will not cure the problem, but a gasket or vacuum hose may.

No specialist can live in a world of his or her own. The mechanic or technician must be able to see and understand the interrelationship of all the parts and integrate them into the whole. Although specialization may be the trend, it is important for the technician to understand the operation of all the other systems in the automobile, heavy equipment, or truck.

THE TURBULENT FUTURE

The near future holds excellent opportunities for the auto repair person. Today there is an urgent need for qualified people. In fact, there is even a need for less-qualified people.

If you get half a dozen people in a room and begin talking about automobile repair, you are bound to get more than one story of despair. You may hear of how someone took a car to the shop and got the bad news that it would not be ready for several days. If the problem was not severe, the person was probably given an appointment for sometime the following week, or even later. There just aren't enough auto repair technicians to go around. And this situation is not expected to change for some time to come. If new hybrid engines are brought into production, the need will grow for people trained in the new technologies.

An even more significant problem today is that there are very few well-qualified technicians. Whenever people find auto technicians they can trust, they stick to them like glue. In fact, this is part of the reason that the public frequently believes that it is being cheated by those in the auto repair business. There is really not very much dishonesty in the field. Problems often occur, however, because the repair people do not fully understand the operation of the vehicle well enough to diagnose problems accurately. When someone blows a diagnosis, the most common thing to do is try to explain to the customer that there is more than one problem and try again. This sort of trial-and-error method of auto repair is not well accepted; especially when the consumer must pay for the mechanic's mistakes. So it is not so much a case of out-and-out cheating as it is of simple ignorance of the totality of the machine that creates the problems and the mistrust.

As much as the motoring public sorely needs good mechanics to fix its cars, it often must settle for marginal work because there are too few experienced and expert technicians available who can do the job. Those who are exceptional can get almost any price they ask for their services. Even if we see a radical shift to a new technology, say, hydrogen fuel cells, the likelihood is that mechanics will still be in great demand.

OUR MOBILE SOCIETY

There is a dire need for more technicians in the near future, and it is expected to remain the same, or even increase, in the next century. Americans love their cars, and they are not about to give them up, no matter how high the cost of fuel gets.

Our whole society is based on mobility. We cannot rely on mass transit to get to everything, nor will we be willing to go everywhere that way in the future. We want our freedom to go where we please, when we please.

As a mobile society, we always will need qualified people to repair our vehicles when they break down. Perhaps we won't recognize the cars of the future. They may be powered by gasoline, solar energy, electricity, propane, alcohol, hydrogen, or any number of other exotic fuels. But no matter how they are powered, professional automotive technicians will be needed to keep them rolling—or perhaps hovering, if that be the case.

The auto repair jobs of the next ten years are likely to be found in dealerships and independent repair shops. Fewer will be in traditional service stations, as more convert to gas/food outlets without road mechanic services.

ADAPTABILITY

It has been the hallmark of the good technician to keep abreast of changing technologies. He or she has adapted from steam to spark ignition and to electronic ignition controlled by black boxes. The technician has no choice but to keep learning, and the top-notch technician will keep up by adapting to whatever technology comes along.

SPECIALIZATION

As mentioned above, the trend is toward specialization in the repair field. If we could look into a crystal ball, we might find that the independent, general mechanic is a dying breed. Already we see that there are many specialization shops in existence—muffler shops, tune-up shops, transmission shops, and alignment shops. According to Gene Gardner, the 1996 president of the Automotive Service Industry Association, "The growth in auto electronics has significantly altered the technical requirements of the individuals who will service these high-tech machines. What this means is that by the turn of the century, those technicians who specialize in learning and understanding these heavily computerized vehicles will be able to diagnose, service, and repair at a level that separates them from others."

Although electronics ranks as a major 1990s change, other trends are also clear. Since the 1970s and 1980s, there has been considerable downsizing of cars, and as a result, there has been an increase in the number of specialty tools needed to repair them. Engines are smaller, transmissions and brake systems are smaller, and engines are being installed transversely in order to power front-wheel-drive cars.

As the vehicles and vehicle systems grow more complex and sophisticated, there is probably going to be a great deal more specialization. Any one person will be hard pressed to understand adequately all the systems and subsystems in the automobile. As mentioned earlier, there are so many engine functions on late-model cars that are handled by electronic controls that there will be a need for specialists in this single area. The computer controls of today are only a fraction of what can, and probably will, be added in the future.

ENGINE SPECIALIST

The dramatic increase in the number of small engines on the road will probably result in more engine failures. In the old trusty V-8, if one spark plug or valve was weak, there was not a significant problem. Only one-eighth of the performance was lost. But today, the four-cylinder engine is common. If the same spark plug or valve should fail, a full 25 percent of the performance is gone. Suddenly, it is a *big* problem.

In addition, most people are driving the smaller engines in the same way that they drove those gigantic gas guzzlers. They push them to the speed limit and beyond and expect them to do the job of a big block. Simple arithmetic tells us that a four-cylinder engine will spin about twice as fast, and make twice as many revolutions to cover the same distance at the same speed, as the V-8. The corollary to this is that a four-cylinder engine will probably wear out sooner. That translates into a need for more engine specialists. There will be more piston rings, more valves, and more camshafts to be replaced.

Along the same lines, the smaller wheels on the downsized cars will revolve more times to cover the same distance. The smaller brakes will have to do a bigger job. So there will be a need for more wheel service—brake jobs, alignments, and wheel-bearing replacements. The extension of this is that there may be a big opportunity for wheel service specialists.

NO MORE TUNE-UPS

Soon we will be seeing the end of the tune-up. It will be replaced by engine performance diagnosis and repair. The tune-up traditionally meant replacing the spark plugs, ignition points, and condenser. Today, there are no points and no condensers. The timing is electronically controlled on most vehicles. All the technician can do is check it and perhaps make an initial minor adjustment. But all of the electronic systems that control every function in the engine have to receive inputs from sensors located in such places as the exhaust, water jacket, and intake manifold. If a sensor is malfunctioning, the performance of the engine will be affected, since the computer will not have the necessary information to make a correction to the performance of the engine. Emissions are one of the factors that these devices are built to control. Another is improved fuel economy. The two, although somewhat opposed, must function hand in hand.

Sophisticated diagnostic instruments analyze the systems so the proper sensor or control can be repaired. This machinery costs a fortune. Only the specialist in engine performance can afford the equipment—and then he or she will have to do many jobs to make the equipment pay for itself. The special tools and equipment will cost even more in the future.

SPECIALTY SHOP VS. GENERAL SHOP

All this talk of specialization does not mean that there will be only specialty shops to handle special problems. In fact, there will still be general shops where the motorist can leave the car and have all the necessary repairs done with one stop, but that shop will probably hire several different technicians, each of whom will specialize. As many as eight or ten specialists in different areas may be necessary. The technicians may be assisted by less experienced helpers who will do the labor. The assistant, or helper, will most likely be an apprentice who eventually will work his or her way into the post of diagnostician. The diagnostician will use specialized equipment to help determine the problem, but only he or she can interpret the data and make the final decisions.

BRIGHT FUTURE

At present there is an urgent need for more trained technicians. In the future, there will be even greater demand. There's room for as many as sixty to eighty thousand more technicians. As those in the field retire or are outpaced by the technology, there will be an even greater need for people to fill the void they leave.

Estimates from the Automotive Service Industries Association (ASIA) indicate that in 1950 there was one mechanic for every 73 cars and trucks. In

1970 there was one mechanic for every 130 vehicles. And, according to the auto repair task force report of the National Association of Attorneys General, in 1995 there was one technician for every 142 cars. According to the Automotive Aftermarket Industry Association (AAIA), "industry estimates put the optimum ratio at one technician for 87 cars and trucks—and we're getting further away from that number with each passing year."

The cost of tools and training continues to escalate, and as such, there are going to be fewer people who can afford to be general automotive technicians. There will be more specialization, more opportunities, and more vehicles on the roads. There will continue to be a great need for skilled professionals who can service these vehicles. There will be more opportunities than people to fill them. Demand will be high and supply low. At least in theory, wages, fringe benefits, and respect will have to increase to attract new talent. For the person who enters the field today, opportunities are almost limitless. If he or she stays abreast of emerging technologies and automotive systems, the sky is the limit.

Beyond the internal combustion engine, there's a world of new technology. Technicians will have to follow these trends and anticipate where they'll lead. Will it be ethanol that replaces oil? Or will hydrogen fuel cells win the day? At this point it's not clear if a new type of engine will be called for. But it's almost certain that within the working lifetimes of today's technicians there'll be a major change; as oil supplies dwindle, new alternatives will be found. A reengineering of the automotive engine, when and if it happens, also would mean the reeducation of the technician workforce. You'll be able to watch these changes happen, and, we hope, be prepared to work with them. Meanwhile, "for the next couple of decades, it is expected by most that petroleum-based fuels will continue to be the primary transportation fuels," wrote Kevin Green, a researcher in the Transportation Strategic Planning and Analysis Office at the Volpe National Transportation Systems Center.

CHAPTER 3

TECHNICIANS—NOT JUST MECHANICS

A technician's most valuable skill is the ability to reason things through based on thorough knowledge of the functions of the automobile. In fact, it is usually a source of pride and a feeling of accomplishment for the technician to diagnose and repair the most difficult and hard-to-find problems.

Whenever something malfunctions in either the engine, drive-train, or electrical system, the technician first gets a description of the problem from the customer. If the technician works in a large shop or automobile dealership, the description may come from the repair order or the service adviser. It is then the technician's duty to test-drive the car to try and determine the possible problem and attempt to narrow it down. He or she then returns to the shop and uses such sophisticated diagnostic equipment as engine analyzers, alignment equipment, compression testers, or gauges to try to isolate the source of the problem. Once the problem is determined, the technician must fix it. Sometimes he or she will repair a component, and other times it will be replaced.

The general automotive technician performs a variety of jobs. Some prefer to specialize. For example, the automatic transmission specialist works on gear trains, couplings, hydraulic pumps, valve bodies, clutch assemblies, and other parts of the automatic transmission. Automatic transmissions are quite complex and require that the technician have a great deal of training. Understanding hydraulics is also vitally important.

The tune-up specialist uses sophisticated equipment to make the engine run at its best. He or she replaces and adjusts the points on older vehicles or inspects and possibly replaces the triggering assemblies of the electronic ignition system on newer cars. The tune-up technician may replace spark plugs, fuel system parts, or

14

emission parts in order to get the engine running properly. He or she also adjusts the valves, the ignition timing (or injection timing on diesel equipped cars), and the fuel injection system for maximum fuel economy and performance. The tune-up technician often uses scientific testing equipment to check and adjust the engine to original manufacturer's specifications.

The automobile air-conditioning specialist not only installs air-conditioning units, but also services and repairs them as necessary. The system must be recharged on a regular basis, and occasionally parts like compressors, lines, evaporators, and condensers have to be replaced.

The alignment specialist or technician most often does wheel alignments. But this type of specialist also is expected to make measurements and determine the wear to front-end parts like struts or springs and shock absorbers and to linkage parts like tie rods, center links, and ball joints. If they are found to be worn beyond specifications, they are replaced.

Brake technicians usually do brake jobs consisting of replacing the linings and machining the brake drums or rotors. They also must understand the principles of hydraulics that actuate the brakes. They repair master cylinders, wheel cylinders, and calipers.

The cooling system technician cleans radiators with caustic solutions and locates and repairs leaks in radiators and heater cores. He or she also may repair gas tanks. The cooling system specialist tests and replaces thermostats, hoses, water pumps, and even a gasket like the head gasket, should it be found to be leaking.

Transmission and driveline technicians test and repair manual transmissions, clutches, and differential assemblies, as well as drive shafts and universal joints.

There are plenty of other jobs that the general technician is expected to do. He or she may be responsible for repairing squeaks and rattles, windshield wipers and washers, window regulators, exhaust systems, power windows, power seats, or any number of other problems.

If there is anything you can think of on a car that could possibly fail or malfunction, it is the job of the general technician to fix or replace it.

GENERAL TECHNICIAN, LIGHT REPAIR

The light repair specialist usually is not responsible for making repairs to the more important systems of the vehicle but may be responsible for checking the car out before delivery at the new car dealership. He or she may install accessories and small parts like rearview mirrors, go over the vehicle, make certain adjustments, and verify that everything is working.

Some of the other items he or she may service are the exhaust system, valve clearance, and brake adjustments. This specialist may be responsible for retorquing the head bolts after major engine work has been performed, checking the timing, inspecting brakes and steering, and making adjustments to various components.

Light repair is a basic stepping-stone to the other more complicated and better-paying positions. Almost all general technicians begin in the area of light repair. It is the training ground for learning more about the overall operation of the vehicle. It offers opportunity to explore the various systems and can lead to a position in heavy repair or to one of the several specialty areas, such as brakes or engine performance or transmissions.

GENERAL TECHNICIAN, HEAVY REPAIR

The heavy repair technician is the person who really digs into the engine, transmission, or differential. He or she is called on to dismantle, inspect, and repair the major components, such as pistons, valves, crankshaft, or camshaft.

Although most of the work done by the heavy repair technician is performed with basic hand tools, large machine tools also may be used. The heavy repair technician may be responsible for removing the entire engine at times, disassembling and rebuilding it as required. The internal mechanics of the engine require that everything be very precise, so the heavy engine technician must use specialty tools like micrometers, dial indicators, and other measuring devices to fit the components precisely.

This specialist also may use machine shop equipment to grind valves and valve seats, plane cylinder heads, and hone cylinder bores. A torque wrench is essential when reassembling to be sure the parts are properly fastened.

The heavy repair specialist must study extensively and have a great deal of practical experience. He or she usually works under the direction and guidance of a qualified and experienced mentor. Success in this field depends largely on the person's natural aptitude, interest, ambition, and a sincere desire to learn. Once he or she has mastered the work involved, the heavy repair specialist will be a valuable asset to any shop and will be in a good position for advancement.

WHERE THEY WORK

There were more than a million auto technicians in 1998 in the United States and about 134,000 in Canada. Some 437,700 were certified by the Institute for Automotive Service Excellence, a national organization formed to improve auto technicians' education. Roughly half of all technicians work in automotive repair shops. Other technicians work in automobile dealerships, service stations, tire stores, and department stores that offer mechanical service. Usually, they work indoors in clean and well-lit shops. However, some older shops may be dim and much dirtier.

Automotive technicians work with their hands and handle many grimy and greasy parts. They may use quite a bit of strength to loosen and remove old parts that may be rusted or seized. Much time is spent leaning over a fender and working on an engine. Much more time is spent under the car while it is on the lift. The work can be strenuous and demanding. Sometimes the technician works from awkward positions. When working under the car, dirt and grime may fall in his or her face. Although most shops are well ventilated, there is usually the odor of gasoline and exhaust in the air.

The picture is not totally bleak, though. Most of the time the technician works independently with little supervision. He or she can walk around during the workday—a healthy aspect of the job! Technicians are not confined to a desk, nor do they usually perform repetitive tasks that can be boring. New problems always come up, and the technician is challenged to use both brawn and brain to solve them. In this way, the work is often satisfying.

Places of employment vary. The technician may work for the federal government, state government, or the military. He or she may work for a fleet like a taxi service or bus or truck line. There are leasing and rental car companies, parcel delivery services, and airport ground equipment companies that the technician may work for. Any firm or organization that uses motorized rolling equipment or machinery also needs the professional automotive technician.

LEARNING THE TRADE AND MOVING UP

Automotive technicians learn much of their craft on the job. Beginners usually start as helpers, lubrication workers, or service station attendants. Gradually, as they acquire more and more skills, they are promoted to more responsible jobs. Although some beginners may be making repairs of a light nature in as little as a few months, it usually takes three to four years to become proficient enough to do most of the common repairs. It may take an additional year or two to learn a specialty.

Most training authorities recommend three or four years of formal training and/or an apprenticeship program. Formal apprenticeship programs may be hard to find. Recently, automotive manufactures banded together to form educational programs based on the European apprenticeship system. Since its founding in 1995, this Auto Youth Educational System program has grown to include some two hundred schools and dealership sponsors, and it's expanding in the United States and Canada. There may be a similar program near you. (See Chapter 13, "Learning the Trade.") These training programs usually combine on-the-job experience with formal classroom instruction. Classroom instruction includes courses in related theory, such as mathematics and physics, as well as such other areas as shop safety practices and customer relations.

For entry-level jobs, employers usually look for young persons with an aptitude for things mechanical and a knowledge of automobiles. Usually a driver's license is required since it is necessary to test-drive vehicles.

Getting your high school diploma is a big advantage in getting an entry-level job. Most employers believe that graduation indicates that a young person has at least some of the traits of a good worker, such as perseverance and the ability to learn, and has the potential for advancement. Courses in automobile repair offered by many high schools also are helpful. In particular, courses in physical science and mathematics can help a person understand how an automobile operates.

Technicians are expected to buy their own hand tools, and beginners are expected to accumulate tools as they gain experience. Many experienced technicians have thousands of dollars worth of tools. The employer usually supplies the larger power tools, specialty tools, and diagnostic equipment.

Sometimes employers send experienced technicians to factory training schools to learn how to repair more recent models or get training in some specialty like automatic transmissions or air-conditioning. Auto manufacturers send representatives to shops on occasion to conduct short training sessions, and many aftermarket manufacturers of parts will conduct training sessions at a local jobber (parts store) or warehouse at little or no charge for professional mechanics who use their products.

Experienced technicians who have leadership or management ability may advance to shop foreman, service adviser, or service manager. Many technicians go on to open their own shop or service station. About one out of five technicians is self-employed.

CHAPTER 4

SERVICE STATION ATTENDANTS

Traditionally, the main entry-level job in automotive service was service station attendant. Although the number of openings in the field is declining, attendants are still in demand. You've probably noticed many self-service islands, but recently there has been some effort to bring back the full-service option. The attendant usually checks the oil, radiator coolant level, battery water, hoses, belts, and other easily accessible items for signs of wear. He or she then advises the customer of the status of everything and suggests having an item serviced, should it be found to be in less-than-acceptable condition.

Besides these basic services, many service stations also offer repair facilities. According to government statistics, there were about 99,000 service stations in 1999. Although about half converted to a food-gas format, the majority are qualified to perform repairs. They employed 141,000 attendants. The scope of repairs may vary from facility to facility, but most offer at least minor repairs and stock replacement items like headlights, windshield wipers, batteries, tires, belts, hoses, and filters. Frequently the attendant is responsible for installing many of these parts and doing minor repair and service work like changing oil and filters, rotating tires, fixing flats, and lubrication. Most of these repairs are performed with such basic hand tools as screwdrivers, wrenches, and pliers. Some attendants are known as technician-attendants and may use more sophisticated equipment, such as engine analyzers and wheel alignment and balancing machines.

The service station attendant also collects the money from the customer for purchases and service. The attendant may be responsible for making out charge sales slips and verifying customers' credit over the telephone for major purchases.

19

The attendant is usually responsible for keeping the building and grounds clean and attractive. He or she may sweep the shop and driveway, clean the rest rooms and the windows, and might also be responsible for stocking shelves, taking inventories, setting up displays, and keeping business records. At the end of the person's shift, he or she is usually responsible for taking sales readings from the gasoline pumps, recording gallons and dollar sales on the pump for his or her shift. The attendant then computes the total sales for the shift, counts the money collected, and balances the books for that shift.

Many service stations also offer emergency road services. The attendant may be responsible for driving a tow truck, boosting dead batteries, changing tires, performing other minor repairs, and towing cars to the station.

WORKING CONDITIONS

Everyone is familiar with the two basic kinds of service stations: those where mechanical repairs and service are performed and those where only motor fuels are dispensed. In both cases, the service station attendant's main duty is to serve the customer at the pump island. Most fulltime attendants work about forty to forty-eight hours per week. Most service stations are open at least six days a week, and some are open every day. The majority of the stations stay open in the evenings, and some may stay open twenty-four hours a day. As a result, the attendant may have a schedule that includes some evenings, weekends, and holidays.

Most of the work is outdoors. Therefore, the attendant must expect to work when the weather is sunny and mild and also when it is raining or snowing. In fact, the attendant is most vital when the weather is bad. At those times, many motorists are reluctant to use a self-service island.

The job of service station attendant is an active one. There is a lot of lifting and stooping, and much time is spent on one's feet.

The attendant greets the customer and dispenses fuel. The dispensing nozzles have an automatic shut-off device built into them. At the full-service island, there is often a locking mechanism that can be engaged so that the attendant need not hold the nozzle until the tank is full. As the fuel is pumped, the attendant may check under the hood, examine the oil level and condition, and check the battery water level and hose and belt conditions at the same time. The attendant acts as a salesperson and attempts to sell a quart of oil or a replacement belt if needed. The attendant checks the tire pressures and adjusts them if necessary.

The service station attendant is at some risk of personal injury. Sharp pieces of metal are inside the engine compartment, and the engine is usually quite hot. If a hose bursts, attendants risk being scalded. Attendants do not often ask to inspect the radiator coolant level unless the engine is cold. Since the coolant is as hot as 200 to 250 degrees and under as much as eighteen pounds of pressure, removing the radiator cap can cause a geyser of hot water and steam to burst forth.

Sometimes the dipsticks for checking the oil and transmission fluid levels are in hard-to-reach places, and one can get scraped knuckles and burned hands when trying to check these items. Batteries produce explosive gases, and gasoline vapors are very volatile. Smoking or sparks from any source can result in violent explosions. The attendant needs to be very safety conscious.

On the plus side for many attendants is the opportunity to deal with a variety of people. In addition, there is the opportunity to work on cars and gain familiarity with them. Many people who start out as attendants aspire to owning or managing their own stations someday.

For the high school student, the service station business provides the easiest option for part-time employment. Many stations do not offer service or mechanical repairs after normal business hours but need trustworthy and courteous employees to handle the fuel business in the evenings and on weekends. It's a way to see if you'd like a full-time job.

PLACES OF EMPLOYMENT

Service stations dot the nation. Wherever there are communities and major highways, there are service stations. According to Department of Labor statistics, there were about 109,050 people working as service station attendants in 1999. About one-third of these were part-time employees. According to a survey done by Super Automotive Service, there were roughly 71,000 service stations in the United States in 1987. In 1999, according to government statistics, there were 99,000 gasoline service stations. Of course, many stations have converted to a food/gas format—about 54,000, or half of the U.S. stations—so fewer mechanics/technicians are hired, but attendants are still needed. Their average wages were $7.58 an hour in 1999.

Service station attendants work in every part of the nation, from the smallest rural communities to the largest metropolitan areas—from the busy, high-volume downtown station to the loneliest station at a remote highway intersection.

QUALIFICATIONS

Applicants for a job as a service station attendant need to meet some basic requirements. They should have a valid driver's license, understand how an automobile works, and be familiar with the operation and location of the various items in the engine compartment. The attendant should know how to examine fluids, belts, and hoses; replace filters and wiper blades; and install oil and transmission fluid.

The service station attendant should have a neat appearance, be friendly and courteous, and like to deal with people. He or she should have a certain degree of self-confidence and be articulate enough to explain things to the customer. It is often important to be a salesperson, and confidence improves the attendant's ability to do so.

The applicant should have good arithmetic skills. The person should be trustworthy and honest. More and more, owners and managers make use of tests to determine the applicant's honesty, since an attendant is responsible for large sums of money.

Most employers prefer high school graduates but will often hire students for part-time employment. A high school education is usually required to take advantage of the management training programs offered by many of the major oil companies.

TRAINING

Most service station attendants receive their training on the job. There are some formal training programs.

Many high schools offer formal training in service station work. For the part-time person, this is the best place to start. Some schools offer a work-study program and will assist in placing the student in a service station. The student may earn scholastic credit for time spent at the service station. The program usually consists of several basic business education and automotive courses. Students usually receive instruction in service station operation in the classroom and put it into practice at the job site.

Some of the major oil companies offer formal training programs. These programs usually take from two to eight weeks to complete. The student is taught simple automotive service and maintenance as well as marketing and business management. Emphasis is usually placed on selling techniques and customer relations. The trainee learns how to take inventory and control the flow of production. He or she also is taught how to order products and display them and how to make sales.

ADVANCEMENT

A multitude of avenues will open to the person who begins as a service station attendant. Once the entry-level attendant becomes familiar with the automobile, he or she may seek training in becoming an automotive technician or mechanic. Most service station mechanics who get formal training go on to work at automobile dealerships or independent garages, or they return to the service station industry to work as full-time technicians.

Those whose talents lean more toward management may eventually become night managers or full-time managers of their own stations. Others may be able to find jobs as service managers or service advisers at automobile dealerships.

Many persons who combine the talents of a mechanic with those of business management aspire to own or manage their own service station. In fact, many mechanics eventually open their own service stations, but unless they also are good at business, or find a partner who is, they may fail. The service station business is one of the easiest to get into but also one of the easiest in which to fail.

Some service stations are owned privately, while others are leased from oil companies. Today there is a shift toward ownership rather than leasing. For some of those who lease, the oil company may eventually be the source of jobs as sales representatives or district managers.

EMPLOYMENT OUTLOOK

Overall employment in the service station industry is expected to remain steady or show a slight decline through the next decade. Projections call for about 139,000 attendants nationwide in 2008, a slight drop from current levels. This is primarily due to an anticipated leveling off of gasoline consumption. Although the public has been driving more, vehicles are becoming more fuel efficient. Another factor is the rise in the number of strictly self-serve facilities that are nothing more than stores that sell fuel and, frequently, convenience food items. Some industry analysts point out that full-service station attrition may have peaked and the service station universe has stabilized.

In any event, the employment outlook is still quite good. Since the service station industry is such a large one, thousands of job openings will become available every year, mostly because former attendants move on to other occupations.

Usually the best way to get more information about becoming a service station attendant is to go directly to a few stations in your area and talk with the manager or other attendants. You may wish to discuss job possibilities with your school guidance counselor or shop instructor. The local state employment service also can be of assistance.

CHAPTER 5

SERVICE ADVISERS AND MANAGERS

When people take their cars in for service, they often deal with a service adviser, the intermediary between the customer and the automotive technician. In most larger repair facilities and automobile dealerships, this person is the link between the customer and technician.

The service adviser finds out from the customer what he or she wishes done. It's essential to get a good description of the problem the motorist is experiencing. This can be a little tricky. If the customer gives the service adviser a weak description of the problem, the adviser may have to quiz the customer to determine what the source of the malfunction might be. He or she also may test-drive the car, either with or without the customer, in an attempt to observe and diagnose the problem. Whenever possible, the service adviser fills out the repair order with a description of the symptoms and may occasionally make a suggestion as to how the problem may be repaired.

The service adviser usually gives the customer an estimate of cost and how long the work is expected to take. Since this is not always possible until a mechanic examines the vehicle, the service adviser may later have to telephone the customer to give the estimates and obtain the customer's approval to have the work done. Sometimes a customer will balk at the cost of repairs and will be reluctant to have the work done. Here the service adviser must convince him or her that having the work performed will be worth it, and the service adviser will have to explain how the work may be vital to the customer's safety, may improve performance, or may prevent some more serious and expensive problem from developing later.

In some of the larger shops and dealerships, a shop dispatcher may compute the estimates and distribute the repair orders to various specialist technicians. In smaller shops, however, the service adviser may perform these duties.

When the customer comes back to pick up the vehicle, the service adviser will answer any questions about the cost of parts and labor and explain in simple terms just what has been done. If there is a complaint, the service adviser is the person who must face the customer. If a repair has been made and the customer returns with a complaint, the service adviser must either see that the repair is redone or obtain management approval to make an adjustment to the customer's bill.

The service adviser is expected to advise customers on routine service requirements, but he or she also may be a salesperson of accessories. Service advisers sometimes suggest accessories that will make driving more pleasurable or safe. They also may instruct the customer as to how he or she should maintain the vehicle. In many shops the service adviser is also the service manager.

WORKING CONDITIONS

Most service advisers put in a forty- to forty-eight hour week. They face two rush periods in the average day. In the morning, most of the customers are dropping their vehicles off for service, and the service adviser must deal with them quickly and politely. Few people have time to spare in the morning, and the service adviser must work at maximum efficiency during this rush period. The second rush period comes in the evening when the customers return to pick up their vehicles. The service adviser has the obligation of delivering the vehicle and explaining the repairs without holding up the rest of the customers.

Most of the service adviser's day is spent standing. However, the work involved is not strenuous physically, even if it is sometimes mentally and emotionally exhausting. Service advisers usually work in clean, well-lit, comfortable conditions indoors. They are usually stationed in the shop area, where it can be noisy. They may sometimes be required to go outdoors to inspect and test-drive vehicles in bad weather.

WHERE TO WORK

There are about 24,400 persons employed as service advisers. Most of them work in larger automobile dealerships with more than twenty employees. In smaller dealerships the service manager doubles as the service adviser. Large independent repair shops need service advisers. In some of the specialty shops the manager of the facility is also the service adviser and occasionally also may perform duties as a service technician.

Usually service advisers receive their training on the job under the guidance of an experienced service adviser or service manager. In most cases, trainees start by assisting the shop dispatcher, or they begin as a porter or car-hiker who drives the vehicles into and out of the shop. Beginners learn how to route the work to the various technicians, compute repair estimates and costs, and estimate the time required to perform the work. It usually takes about one or two years to become proficient enough to handle the job well. Some service advisers attend vocational schools or community and junior colleges and take auto mechanics courses to get an understanding of vehicles. This enables them to be conversant and knowledgeable when dealing with both technicians and customers.

Most employers prefer high school graduates who are at least twenty-one years of age. It is extremely helpful to have experience or training in automotive repair and related activities. Employers often fill vacancies for the automotive service adviser by promoting from within the organization. The person promoted may have worked as a mechanic trainee or parts counter trainee, although many firms prefer to hire someone who is well versed in all areas of automotive service repair.

During high school you should consider taking classes in grammar and English, along with general mathematics, public speaking, commercial or business mathematics, and automobile mechanics. Unless you are quite familiar with automotive service, vocational or technical school is advised.

Since the service adviser is the intermediary between the public and the technicians, employers look for men or women who are gregarious and who can win customer confidence, as customer confidence is the key to repeat business. Employers look for persons who are neat, courteous, even-tempered, good listeners, and good conversationalists.

If a service adviser has any supervisory or managerial experience, he or she may be a good candidate for a service manager position. Some service advisers who have good mechanical skills and keen business sense go on to open their own repair shops or service stations.

CURRENT OUTLOOK

The field of service adviser occupations is rather small compared to others in the automotive services. According to the United States Department of Labor, the outlook for the near future is better than average for service sales representatives.

Openings usually come from normal attrition, as some who are presently employed retire, die, or move on to some other job. The number of annual openings is expected to grow as the vehicle population grows. This job is relatively unaffected by changing economic conditions. Most of the openings for service advisers will be concentrated in the larger metropolitan areas where the larger dealerships and repair shops are found.

CHAPTER 6

RECYCLERS AND DISMANTLERS

If you are calling these places junkyards, you are living in the past. Today this huge and growing industry is known as automotive dismantling and recycling. Perhaps you have never given it much thought, but a career in the automotive dismantling and recycling industry could be a great opportunity. It may be hard to believe, but today it is the sixteenth largest industry in the United States. There are two thousand member companies in the Automotive Recyclers Association, all part of an industry with $8.2 billion in annual sales (www.autorecyc.org). Business is booming, and there is plenty of room for a lot of people.

There is dignity in being an automotive dismantler. You will be doing something worthwhile for both yourself and your community. By recycling, we conserve energy and natural resources. The price of repairs, which is generally high, can be kept lower by using salvaged parts.

As the costs of collision and mechanical repairs go up, more and more insurance companies are requesting that recycled parts be used whenever possible. On the face of it, this may seem unfair, but in the long run, it may help to keep everyone's insurance rates within reason. Americans are beginning to realize the necessity of recycling in many ways, from paper to glass to metals. The automotive recycling industry has understood how important it is for many years.

DISMANTLER

The dismantler's job is to take a car or truck apart carefully and identify each part so that it can be put in inventory or sent directly to the sales counter upon request. The dismantler uses a variety of basic hand tools, such as wrenches and screwdrivers, in addition to cutting torches and power saws and a variety of lifts and machinery. It takes a lot of ingenuity to get specific parts off a damaged and twisted vehicle, and every usable piece must be salvaged whenever possible.

INVENTORY CONTROL PERSON

Once the dismantler gets the parts off, they go to an inventory control person who is responsible for keeping track of every available used part. This person is responsible for inventorying major parts, usually via computer, and is therefore vital to the business. He or she keeps records of what has been sold and any items that may be needed or on order.

The inventory control person must be good with details and must keep accurate records, which may be as simple as a neat card file or as complex as a computerized system. Efficiency is the key to a superior inventory control system.

SALESPERSON

Another vital link in the recycling business is the salesperson. He or she may be an outside salesperson who is on the road visiting body shops, new car dealers, or garages and service stations. Or he or she may be a counter salesperson who handles sales either in person or over the phone. A salesperson must enjoy working with many other people.

MANAGEMENT

Most of the automotive recycling establishments are small businesses that are individually owned. The owner usually manages the operation, but sometimes a general manager is needed as the business grows. The annual gross sales in the typical automotive recycling business are below $500,000. It is the responsibility of management to keep the business operating profitably so that it can grow and salary and wage increases can he awarded. If you desire to become a member of management, it is important to learn to operate as productively as though the business were your own.

OTHER OPPORTUNITIES

There are a myriad of other positions available in the auto recycling industry. There is a need for forklift operators, truck drivers, warehouse stock persons, office managers, administrative assistants, sales managers, and many, many more. As with any small company, often many jobs are combined. But in large companies, they may be separate.

Some operations specialize in a particular area of recycling. One business may deal only in import parts, while another may specialize in one make or model of car, like only Buicks or exclusively Corvettes. Others may deal specifically with motorcycle parts. Automotive recycling is a big business, and it is growing. About six thousand recycling shops in the United States employ forty-six thousand workers. They recycled 4.7 million vehicles in 1997, according to the ARA.

For more information on the opportunities in the field of automotive recycling, contact:

Automotive Recyclers Association
3975 Fair Ridge Drive
Suite 20, North
Fairfax, VA 22033-2924

CHAPTER 7

PARTS SPECIALISTS

Automobile parts must be replaced from time to time to keep the vehicle in good working order, work that keeps about one hundred thousand persons employed as auto parts counter workers.

Most auto parts and supplies counter workers are employed by wholesale and retail automobile parts stores (usually referred to as *jobbers* in the trade) and automobile dealerships. The people who work in retail and wholesale parts stores sell parts for a wide variety of makes and models of cars and trucks. Their customers are usually independent repair shops, service stations, self-employed technicians, and "do-it-yourselfers." The counter workers in dealerships handle only the parts and supplies for the particular line of vehicles sold by the dealership. They spend most of their time dealing with the technicians and providing the part or parts requested by those technicians.

SKILLS REQUIRED

Parts stores and dealerships stock literally thousands of parts, and the counter worker must become familiar with most of them on sight to identify and locate the parts quickly for customers. Sometimes the customer may give only a vague description of the part needed, and the counter person must be able to determine what part is being requested. Especially at the retail level, the customer may ask for a "gizmo that connects to the intake manifold" and try to describe what it looks like. Since most of the time the customer telephones the store, the counter person might have to determine what the caller wants, look up the part in a catalog or a computer, and then check inventory to verify that the part is in stock. All this requires the counter person to have a thorough knowledge of the parts catalogs and the stockroom.

Once the counter person obtains the necessary item, he or she must check the price lists, collect the money from the customer, or fill out the billing forms.

Sometimes the necessary part is not in stock. In these cases, the counter person will have to check for an interchangeable part or place a special order. It may even be necessary to suggest another dealer.

Often the customer—especially the do-it-yourselfer—has no idea what is wrong with the vehicle. The above-average counter person needs a good working knowledge of automobile mechanics and must be able to assist the customer in determining the problem and to suggest the part or parts needed to make the repair. Sometimes the counter person asks the customer to bring in the suspected malfunctioning part for examination. In some instances he or she may use special equipment to test the part, such as coil and condenser testers, spark plug testers, or other measuring instruments.

The parts counter person is often responsible for keeping catalogs and price lists up-to-date. He or she may stock shelves, unpack boxes, take inventories, place orders with suppliers, and set up displays for walk-in clientele.

Many of the larger supply stores may maintain a machine shop. Here they will resurface brake drums and disc brake rotors. Other shops have drill presses, hydraulic presses, cylinder head refacing equipment, valve-grinding machines, and more. Although some stores employ full-time machinists, in many businesses the counter person has a chance to learn those skills too.

WORKING CONDITIONS

Automotive parts and supplies counter workers usually work in clean, well-lit stockrooms where they enjoy air-conditioning as well as comfortable heating. Although most of the work is not physically strenuous, counter workers will spend a lot of the day on their feet. There is also a great deal of walking. Some of the parts may be quite heavy. There is some lifting involved. Unpacking incoming shipments can be a little strenuous at times.

If the counter person also performs machine-shop work, he or she will use basic hand tools as well as special equipment. Although counter work is basically clean, machine-shop work requires handling greasy and soiled components.

Since many people need their vehicles during the week for work, it is usually necessary for those in the automotive industry to work on Saturdays, Sundays, or both. When it is busy, there may be some strain from dealing with the public—especially some of the more difficult customers or those who may need a good deal of advice. More and more parts and supply stores stay open in the evening for the convenience of their customers.

OUTSIDE SALES

Often parts stores develop special arrangements with several local repair shops or service stations. These preferred customers often stock many of the fast-moving parts at their place of business, since they cannot waste time running to the store or waiting for delivery of each and every part they need. If the store has such an arrangement, a counter person also may work as an outside salesperson, visiting the repair shop on a regular basis, usually once a week, and inventorying the repair shop's stock. The salesperson then makes a list of the required items, reviews the list with the owner or manager of the shop, and returns to the store to fill the order. This gives the counter person some degree of mobility and freedom from the routine found in the store. This same person may be responsible for visiting other repair shops and developing new accounts. Preferred customers usually get special discount percentages from the regular prices, and the counter person computes the discount.

PLACES OF EMPLOYMENT

According to the United States Department of Labor, about one hundred thousand persons are employed as automotive counter workers. Most of them are employed by automobile dealers and retail automotive parts stores. The rest of the employers include wholesalers and distributors of automotive parts.

Although trucking companies, bus lines, and fleets that have their own technicians and shops also employ counter persons, these businesses usually do not sell to the public. There are opportunities for employment with these businesses, particularly in the retail and wholesale markets.

Almost anywhere in the country where automotive service is performed, there are parts stores. Since automobile dealerships, repair shops, and service stations are found throughout the nation, employment for automotive counter persons is also nationwide. People who work for trucking companies, bus lines, and fleets, however, are employed mainly in larger cities. The government reported that there were 164,360 auto repair shops and 98,846 gasoline service stations in the United States, based on the latest economic census. In addition there were 22,250 motor vehicle dealers, according to the national Automobile Dealers Association. That means there are almost 300,000 places in business that need parts and supplies. According to the AAIA, "today's U.S. motor vehicle aftermarket is a $250 billion industry employing millions of Americans at more than 500,000 business locations."

TRAINING AND QUALIFICATIONS

Most automotive parts counter persons learn the trade through on-the-job training. Beginners usually start as parts delivery persons or trainees. Sometimes they get started as stock or receiving clerks and work their way up.

Since most entry-level workers begin as stock persons, they eventually become acquainted with their inventory and gradually familiarize themselves with the layout of the stockroom, the catalogs, and price lists. In as little as two or three months they may begin waiting on customers, but it usually takes at least two years to become proficient enough to handle all the various aspects of the job well.

For the most part, employers prefer high school graduates. Occasionally, a student is able to get a part-time job after school or on weekends as a stock clerk. In any event it is best to have some knowledge of automobiles and an interest in how they operate and are repaired.

The high school student should be sure to take mathematics courses, as well as courses in auto mechanics, merchandising, selling, bookkeeping, and even typing. It is important to be able to spell and to have good grammar. It is also helpful to get some practical experience by working on cars and light trucks.

Working at a service station, repair shop, or even as a hobby is invaluable in helping you to gain knowledge.

Automotive parts counter workers will spend a great deal of time dealing with the public. Therefore, it is important to have a neat appearance, to be friendly, and—often—to be tactful. A good memory and an ability to write legibly are important skills to have.

ADVANCEMENT

If you have any supervisory skills or management training or experience, you will probably become a parts department manager or store manager. If you are exceptionally good at dealing with the public, you may be interested in outside sales. The ever-popular dream of owning your own business often comes true for the person with good business sense and ambition.

EMPLOYMENT OUTLOOK

The United States Department of Labor expects the outlook for automotive counter workers to remain constant through 2008. It is an almost recession-proof industry. Whenever the economy is down, fewer new cars are purchased. As a result, many older cars are being driven longer, and that means more parts are going to wear out and fail. In 1996, the average car age was 8.6 years. The Department of Labor indicates that the automobile replacement parts industry is somewhat immune from changing economic conditions and demand is steady. Openings are expected to be created when workers retire or transfer to some other occupation.

The future growth of the automotive parts and supplies industry is difficult to forecast. Future technological developments, such as the use of parts that are more durable, may indeed slow the growth in demand for replacement parts. On the other hand, this same technology is already creating a need for exclusively new parts, since many of the old ones are incompatible with the cars being built today. As an example, the automotive air-conditioning systems that were used for many years are no longer compatible with the new ones.

CHAPTER 8

BODY REPAIR TECHNICIANS

Hundreds of thousands of motor vehicles are damaged every year in America. All sorts of things happen to damage cars and trucks, but the most frequent cause is a traffic accident. Although some of these vehicles will be "totaled" or beyond repair, most can be made to look and perform as if they were brand new. This job is performed by collision repair technicians. They do more than make the outside look good. They remove dents, of course, but they also straighten frames and replace any damaged parts. Although they can usually fix just about any type of vehicle, they work mainly on cars and light trucks. There are a few specialists who work mainly on trucks and buses or trailers.

The first step is preparing the estimate. Whenever a motorist brings his or her car into the shop, the body specialist examines it carefully and notes all the parts that have to be fixed or replaced. He or she then figures the time it should take to do the job. After determining the price of the parts and labor, he or she presents the customer with the estimate. Most body shops have special books and catalogs to help calculate the estimate.

NATURE OF THE WORK

Automobile body specialists use a variety of equipment in their job. To restore bent frames to their original shape, the specialist uses hydraulic machines that are chained to the vehicle in order to twist it back into its original shape.

Once the frame is straightened the damaged body parts are repaired. The body repairer uses a pneumatic cutter, saw, or acetylene torch to remove the sections of the body that are badly damaged. He or she then welds or brazes new sections into place. If a section is only dented, a slide hammer or a variety of specially designed body hammers may be used to return the dent as nearly as possible to its original contour. Sometimes the specialist corrects small dents or creases by hammering on one side of the panel while holding an anvil on the other. Body repairers use special pick hammers and punches to remove tiny dents and pin holes.

Once the sheet metal is restored as nearly as possible to the original shape, the body repair person fills the remaining dents with plastic body filler or solder. The filler material then is filed or sanded before it is painted. In some of the smaller shops the body repair specialist also may do the painting, but often this is done by the painting specialist.

If variety is the spice of life, then body repair must be a pretty spicy job. Each damaged car presents a new challenge, and there are usually many different problems. The specialist typically develops special methods to handle the variety of different problems. The occupation of body repair specialist is one that offers both challenge and pride. The body repairer is a skilled artisan—not unlike a sculptor in many ways.

WORKING CONDITIONS

Most body repair persons work by themselves and get only general instructions from their supervisor. In some shops they may have an assistant or a helper or apprentice. In some of the larger shops the repair technician may specialize in one area, such as fenders or frame straightening.

Almost all the work is done indoors. However, it is not an easy job. Many times the body repairer has to work in an awkward position or in tight areas. The work is both strenuous and dirty. Although most of the shops are very well ventilated, the conditions are usually dusty, and there is often a heavy odor of paint in the air. The automobile body repair shop can be a very noisy place. The whir of power tools for grinding and sanding is almost constant, and there are plenty of hammers banging most of the time.

There are also numerous chances to get injured. Cuts from jagged sheet metal are common. There is the potential for burns from torches and heated metal, and the power tools pose an additional threat. Respiratory problems can develop if the worker does not use a protective breathing mask over the nose and mouth.

PLACES OF EMPLOYMENT

There were about 240,000 persons employed in the automobile body repair trade in 1999. The industry association I-CAR puts the number of technicians at 208,000, working in about 52,700 shops, which generate more than $20 billion in annual sales and repairs by census estimates. Most of them worked in shops that specialize in collision repair service or at automobile dealerships. Some fleets, such as trucking companies and taxi companies, have their own staff of body repair specialists. A large portion of the body specialists work for the vehicle manufacturers on assembly lines. Fit and finish is becoming increasingly important in new cars as the buying public demands better products.

Automobile body repair specialists work everywhere in the country. The opportunities are distributed about the same as the vehicle population.

QUALIFICATIONS

There are not many special qualifications to becoming an auto body specialist. The most important thing is good health, since it is a strenuous occupation. Most employers prefer high school graduates. The body repair specialist needs a keen sense of shape and must be able to work well with his or her hands. Good coordination is a must.

The ability to use tools is also important. Auto body repair persons are usually required to buy their own hand tools as well as the basic power tools that are used every day. The shop, however, usually supplies the large power tools like frame straighteners. The average body repair person spends more than $2,000 for tools over a period of time. Persons usually accumulate their tools as they gain experience. In a few cases the shop will supply the necessary hand tools.

TRAINING

Many body repair specialists learn their trade on the job. They usually enter the field as helpers and will at first do many of the repetitive tasks such as sanding. They then advance to removing damaged parts and replacing them with new or repaired parts. Gradually they are assigned to repair small dents and scratches, and finally they learn to straighten frames.

It takes about three to four years of experience and on-the-job training to become skilled. Most places of employment require three to four years of apprenticeship. Unfortunately, there are not enough places to get this necessary apprenticeship training. There are a few programs available. Apprenticeship includes both on-the-job learning and classroom instruction where safety procedures, mathematics, and business practices are covered.

Courses in auto body repair are offered in some fourteen hundred high schools and colleges. Many of them are certified by the National Automative Technicians Education Foundation (NATEF). The I-CAR Educational Foundation promotes education programs. Top dollar in the field usually goes to formally trained technicians.

ADVANCEMENT

There are not many avenues for advancement in this occupation, which is pretty much a singular craft. Body repair specialists with supervisory ability may be promoted to shop foreman or shop manager. Many of the body specialists go on to open their own shops, and the percentage of auto body specialists who are self-employed is quite high.

Some automobile body repair specialists find excitement in customizing cars, but the market is not very large. Mostly, these persons make custom cars for themselves and a small, select group of customers. Another possible avenue is building special bodies for racing cars. In this case the body specialist may design and build the race car body from scratch. It takes a lot of mathematics and understanding of physics to design a car body for an Indy-type car. Air-flow and ground-effects principles must be calculated into the design. The United States Automobile Club (USAC) and other racing organizations all have specific rules and guidelines that must be strictly followed for safety and performance. An understanding of stress and the ability to design proper reinforcements into the body are critical.

EMPLOYMENT OUTLOOK

According to the United States Department of Labor, employment of automobile body repairers is expected to grow as fast as most professions through 2008, as a result of increase in the number of motor vehicles that will be damaged in traffic and the total number of cars on the roads. Accidents are expected to increase proportionately in spite of improved highways and better bumpers and safety features being built into vehicles.

Most people who enter the occupation should expect rather steady employment, since the automobile repair business is not very sensitive to changing economic conditions, according to the Department of Labor. However, when the economy is slow, many car owners are reluctant to spend money on cosmetic repairs to their cars.

According to the I-CAR Education Foundation, the skills you need to be a body technician include the ability to:

- remove and replace bolt-on parts
- remove and install exterior trim
- align bolt-on panels
- repair and install interior trim
- apply corrosion protection
- replace moveable glass
- disassemble major parts
- repair large dents
- finish body filler with 180 grit
- use MIG welder

The skills you need to be a structural technician include the ability to:

- use MIG welder
- measure/analyze structure damage
- remove structural parts
- disassemble major bolt-on parts
- fit and weld structural parts
- assemble major bolt-on parts
- fit and weld cosmetic parts
- remove welded cosmetic parts
- repair major structure damage

For more information, contact:
I-CAR Education Foundation
3701 Algonquin Road, Suite 400
Rolling Meadows, IL 60008
www.i-car.com

National Automotive Technicians Education Foundation (NATEF)
13505 Dulles Technology Drive
Herndon, VA 20171-3421
www.natef.org

CHAPTER 9

PAINTERS AND REFINISHERS

Automobile painters are skilled workers who take an old vehicle and make it look like new. They're sometimes called refinish technicians.

Painters are often required to mix paints in order to get just the right shade to match the original finish.

The painter must sand the area to remove any old paint, primer, or rust, and repair small areas with solder or plastic body filler. The sanding is done with power tools and by hand. Anything that is not to be painted is masked off with paper and tape.

Once the preparation is done, the painter uses a spray gun to apply several coats of primer to the bare metal. He or she then lightly sands the primed surface, applies several coats of final color, and blends it in with the vehicle's original paint.

The car is dried in a special room where heat lamps speed up the process. (On some vehicles this cannot be done, because the heat can damage some of the on-board computers.)

WORKING CONDITIONS

Automobile painters work indoors in an environment free of contaminants that could settle on the fresh paint. However, they may be exposed to many fumes and vapors that are harmful. Often a special room is provided with ventilated booths to protect the workers, but if it is not, the painters must wear respirators to protect nose and mouth.

Skills you need to be a refinish technician include the ability to:

• featheredge
• mask for urethane, prime, and prep
• prepare and trim parts
• apply guidecoat and block sand
• mask for spot repair
• mask for overall color
• select and apply primer/sealer
• wet sand for overall color
• pressure wash and prep
• apply corrosion protection

PLACES OF EMPLOYMENT

Of the twelve thousand persons working as automobile painters in the 1990s two-thirds of them worked in shops that specialized in auto repairs. The remainder mostly worked for auto or truck dealerships and for fleets that maintain and repair their own vehicles. Although painters work throughout the country, they are mostly concentrated in metropolitan areas.

TRAINING AND QUALIFICATIONS

Training for the automobile painter is usually not formal. Instead it takes the form of learning as a helper to an experienced painter. It usually takes about three or four years to become skilled.

A small number learn through apprenticeship programs. The term of apprenticeship is usually three years, and the student learns on the job and supplements this with classroom work.

Good health, keen eyesight, and a good sense of color are needed. A high school diploma is helpful.

According to the *Occupational Outlook Handbook,* employment of automobile painters is growing a little more slowly than average, and the outlook through 2008 is best for skilled automotive refinishers and transportation equipment painters. Salaries are sometimes supplemented with commission income. Wages average between $10.86 and $18.95 an hour for most workers. The highest wages are about $23.00 an hour.

OTHER RESPONSIBILITIES

Since vehicles that require painting are often damaged due to collision, painters may be required to know how to repair sheet metal. They may personally, or in close cooperation with mechanics, repair some other vehicle components or systems. This is especially true in smaller repair shops that do not employ full-time mechanics.

CHAPTER 10

DIESEL/TRUCK TECHNICIANS

Trucks haul the nation's freight from seaports, rail yards, and airports to the point of use. One of the most complex impressive mechanisms on the road is the Class 8 tractor-trailer rig. The diesel engine and drive train that powers this vehicle has to pull thirty-three thousand pounds and more along the highway, over the mountains, and through the desert if called on to do so. If it's going to last the five hundred thousand miles or more that its owners expect from it, it's going to need to be in good repair. Keeping the nation's truck fleets running is a full-time job in this era of just-in-time inventory and national distribution of merchandise. For those who are up to the challenge, it can be a good career, and demand is high. (For an inside look at the business of trucking and truck maintenance, take a look at VGM's *Opportunities in Trucking Careers*, by Ken Scharnberg, himself a trucker/teacher.)

TRUCK AND BUS TECHNICIAN

Truck and bus technicians who work for truck fleet operations spend much of their time doing maintenance and routine services to ensure that the vehicles do not break down on the road. Maintenance checks usually involve inspection of fluids, steering mechanisms, brakes, wheel bearings, and other important parts. Items that cannot be adjusted or repaired are replaced.

Most truck and bus mechanics are generalists, but in some of the larger fleet shops they may specialize. Sometimes the technicians work as teams.

Since parts on trucks and buses are usually quite a bit larger than similar parts found on cars, the work is harder and takes a bit more muscle. But technicians often can work in teams or with apprentices to get the job done.

45

Most jobs for truck and bus technicians are found in large metropolitan areas, but there is a great need to staff the numerous truck stops and dealerships across the country.

Almost all fleet vehicles are built to the company's specifications, and it is usually the job of the head mechanic to select engine, transmission lights, and even the type of bolts to be used. The head mechanic also determines how the various parts should be installed to make the servicing job faster and easier and to keep downtime to a minimum. The truck manufacturer builds the vehicles to this person's specifications.

There were 255,000 diesel mechanics in 1998. Most ply their trade as truck and bus mechanics. The majority of the truck mechanics work for fleet shops that serve companies large and small, from over-the-road trucking firms, to bakeries and delivery services. Other options are municipal fleets, with their plows, forestry, and streets and sanitation vehicles; distributors; wholesalers; and so on. Of the estimated twenty-five thousand bus mechanics, most work for local transit companies and school bus companies. School bus technicians are a special segment of the craft, and starting in 1996, they were recognized by the National Institute for Automotive Service Excellence (ASE) with a separate certification.

DIESEL SPECIALIST

Almost everything about the diesel engine is the same as a gasoline engine except for the ignition system. There are no spark plugs, but there are glow plugs. There is no ignition distributor, but there is a fuel distributor.

Diesel specialists use all the same basic hand tools as any other type of technician, but they also will employ different diagnostic equipment for service.

They use jacks and hoists, which help them cope with heavy parts. Machinists will use lathes and grinding equipment to rebuild engines, brakes, and other systems. Welding and flame-cutting tools help with metal work, such as replacing exhaust systems.

WHERE DIESEL/TRUCK TECHNICIANS WORK

Diesel technicians may go to work for fleet owners, dealerships, or for independent shops, just like auto technicians. They usually work in a bigger shop, with more room for the heavy trucks. The work is mostly indoors, except if they're called out to repair a truck on the road. According to *Heavy Truck Systems*, by Ian Norman, et al. (Albany, NY: Delmar Publishing, 1996), nearly 40 percent of the trucks in the country are part of large fleets of more than five hundred trucks. Many more are owned by small companies: fleets of one hundred or fewer cover half of all trucks; fleets of ten or fewer account for about 20 percent. The owner-operator is a lesser factor, with about 1 to 5 percent of the marketplace. In a larger shop, there's more specialization among the technicians. In small shops, technicians have to do many tasks, from repair to preventive maintenance.

Because the working life of a truck is so demanding, it is kept on a rigorous maintenance schedule, with checklists and overhauls carefully planned. In large shops, service managers or shop supervisors give assignments to each technician. The supervisors help diagnose the problems and plan repairs, so that quality standards can be met. Electronic diagnostics are making that part of the job easier, once the technician is familiar with the computer and its software.

TRAINING

Because trucks and diesels are a special class of engines, and because they can be part of complex systems in tractor-trailer vehicles, training is specialized. Some high schools offer diesel engine training, but more often the advanced training is given at the community college level. Diesel engine companies help sponsor these programs, as well as continuing education efforts. The trucking companies themselves train technicians on their own customized fleet. The National Institute for Automotive Service Excellence (ASE) in Herndon, VA, handles voluntary certification programs for new graduates and recertification of working technicians every few years.

Many college technical education programs are on the lookout for good students. Enrollment and progress in a certificate program can lead quickly to an internship or an apprenticeship with a local shop. A six-month to two-year program is a good start, with a certificate or an associate degree. Then there's a period of on-the-job training or apprenticeship. In the shop, beginners clean parts at the wash rack and fuel and grease trucks and trailers. They work their way up to the tougher and more interesting repairs. A commercial driver's license is required to test-drive the trucks.

The Bureau of Labor Statistics reports that a journeyman truck technician has usually spent at least three or four years working up to the more difficult tasks. Professionals say that high school students should try to take courses in math and physics and electronics if they're offered, not just automotive repair, if they want to be ready for the intensive truck training that's needed with today's fleets. Good reading skills help, too, when trying to digest a variety of service manuals, software instructions, and so on. Practical experience with automobile repair at a gas station, in the military, or at home is considered a big plus.

Blackhawk Technical College in Wisconsin is one school that offers a program for Diesel and Heavy Equipment Technician. "The program is classroom and shop training in diesel shop practice, diesel engine principles, diesel engine overhaul, fuel systems, heavy duty hydraulic and electrical systems, and diesel engine auxiliary systems," says the school's course description. Graduates have gone on to be engine maintenance specialists, tune-up mechanics, farm equipment mechanics, as well as truck mechanics.

An internship with a company while you are working can lead to a job in the same company when you graduate. Then your employer may pay for more training, so you can specialize in their fleet vehicles, says Kurt Hornicek, director of medium/heavy vehicle technical services at ASE. One advantage of continued training and certification through ASE, he says, is the possibility of advancement and higher salaries, with $50,000 not uncommon for certified truck technicians.

ADVANCEMENT

Trainees move up gradually from entry level to journeyman. In larger shops, there may be a lead tech or supervisor position. Shop foreman or shift supervisor is another possible promotion. Service managers, who deal with managing the work flow, also have some seniority and opportunity for greater compensation. A master technician who's a good communicator may become a corporate trainer, too.

OUTLOOK

Most industry publications, such as *Heavy Duty Trucking* and *Fleet Owner,* are voicing concern about the need for more truck technicians. They see a crisis-level shortage developing, one that the labor statistics aren't yet reflecting. For its part, the government's labor forecasting economists predict a 10 percent increase in employment by 2008. Is it an increase or a crisis? Either way, one good thing is that pay will rise for the technicians who enter the field and stay. Those who are qualified can write their own ticket to a career. The government's best guess is that we'll need 280,000 bus and truck mechanics and diesel engine specialists by 2008. Industry observers worry that with all the retirements and with fewer students entering the field, we won't have enough trainees to fill the bays. So, it's a field waiting for talented newcomers. Wages now are averaging just over $15 an hour, with the top 10 percent of technicians pulling down $21.50 an hour, or about $45,000 a year.

CHAPTER 11

OTHER CAREER SPECIALISTS

Often a person will be a specialist in one or more disciplines within the field. For example, an alignment specialist may be a brake specialist as well. A rare breed of technicians will devote their entire careers to a single area and excel in it as few others can. But it is often advantageous to specialize in at least two areas to be sure that there will always be some work to do.

CLEANING SPECIALIST

Before a used car is sold, it is usually cleaned up to make it more attractive. The person responsible for this work is usually known as a *detailer.* He or she often steam cleans both the engine and the underbody. The detailer also may wash and wax the exterior, vacuum the interior, remove stains, and clean soiled upholstery. The cleaning specialist uses a variety of chemicals to restore the interior and exterior to make the car more appealing to buyers.

The detailer also may pick up and deliver cars to customers or to service technicians in the shop and may test-drive the vehicle after it has been serviced.

The detailer must work independently. He or she usually needs a driver's license but little formal training. There are plenty of chances to observe other work being performed, and with initiative and a desire to learn, the person in this job may advance to another area of service.

BRAKE SPECIALIST

Brake specialists are expected to understand fully the braking system of the automobile. Motorist and passenger safety depends on proper operation of the braking system, and brake specialists have a grave responsibility. People's lives are in their hands.

Today's brake mechanic must understand both the drum and disc braking system as well as the parking brake system and hydraulic system. Computer-controlled antilock brake systems are popular and will be even more so in the future.

The basic job function involves inspecting and replacing brake shoes and disc pads. The brake specialist uses a lathe to machine perfect surfaces on both drums and rotors (discs) and must use micrometers to determine if the parts are serviceable and able to be reinstalled on the vehicle. The brake specialist not only inspects them for wear but also uses tools like a dial indicator to determine if the parts have any lateral or radial runout. This requires precision and attention to detail.

Brake specialists also must understand the principles of hydraulics. They inspect for failures and related problems and rebuild wheel cylinders, calipers, and master cylinders in the braking system. They also inspect and troubleshoot the control devices in the system, such as the proportioning valve or metering valve, which control hydraulic pressures to the different positions of the braking system.

The brake specialist is expected to replace hydraulic fluid lines and hoses when leaks are found. Much like a plumber, he or she makes new lines from stock and bends and joins them to make safe unions with existing parts.

He or she also diagnoses problems and repairs them in the power boosting units, which may be operated by engine vacuum, hydraulics, or in the case of some larger vehicles, air brake compressors.

Before releasing the vehicle to the customer the brake specialist adjusts the brakes, bleeds the system, and road tests the vehicle to be sure it is safe.

LUBRICATION SPECIALIST

The lubrication specialist is responsible for lubricating the working parts of the vehicle. He or she must check fluid levels in the crankcase, transmission, brake master cylinder, and other areas. He or she also may inspect the radiator, differential, and battery. The lube specialist lubricates the front-end parts using specialized equipment while watching for worn or damaged parts.

As they become more proficient, lubrication specialists may be called upon to make critical measurements of components for excessive wear. They usually are responsible for making a safety inspection of other components, such as brake linings, fuel and brake lines, and tires.

There has been a great increase of independent lubrication shops that specialize in quick lubrication service. For the convenience of the motorist, the oil and filter are usually changed and the front end lubricated while the customer waits.

The lube specialist has the opportunity to learn about many of the basic systems, and this familiarity can be a stepping-stone to advancement to more complicated and responsible service.

ALIGNMENT SPECIALIST

The alignment specialist is responsible for making sure the vehicle steers and handles properly.

Alignment technicians must learn to use alignment equipment to determine if the vehicle is tracking properly. They inspect for caster, camber, and toe. These are the names for the three geometric angles of alignment, thus an understanding of geometry is important. Although usually referred to as front-end alignment, the entire vehicle's total geometry is becoming very important with smaller cars. There is a phenomenon known as "rear axle steer" that is becoming very important, especially in smaller cars. The technician will correct the rear axle geometry for total vehicle alignment.

The systems that the alignment specialist must understand include the suspension, steering gearbox or rack-and-pinion assembly, steering linkage, spindles, wheel bearings, and shock absorbers. He or she uses precise diagnostic tools to make determinations for wear and then repairs or replaces defective parts.

When it comes to steering, the alignment specialist has quite a bit to understand on repair. There are two basic types of steering being used on today's cars—recirculating ball and rack-and-pinion. The recirculating ball system has been used on American cars for many years. Most people refer to the device as the "steering box." The second type of steering is rack-and-pinion. This system was once most popular on imported sports cars, but since American cars are getting smaller, it is used much more frequently in the vehicles coming from Detroit.

Wheel balance is another important part of the job. Sophisticated balancing equipment is used to make sure the car rides smoothly at all speeds and to prevent premature tire wear.

The alignment specialist replaces shock absorbers, using a variety of special tools for removal and installation.

The McPherson strut is fast becoming the dominant front suspension system, because it takes up much less space. As the cars get smaller, the strut system is used more and more. The alignment specialist rebuilds the McPherson strut assembly, and after reinstalling it, corrects the vehicle geometry.

The alignment specialty field is growing very rapidly. Once popular in the 1950s, it waned for many years. Now the alignment specialty shop is again coming into vogue.

TOWING AND ROAD SERVICE

Sooner or later almost everyone will require the services of the tow truck or road service person. Persons interested in road service must have a driver's license, and in most states, a special designation may be required for those who operate heavy trucks.

Most road service people should have a working knowledge of minor repairs and should understand the basics of ignition and fuel systems. It is mainly an outside job, and the person should be prepared to work during bad weather and unusual hours or to be on call.

Most towing or road service companies are small businesses with fewer than three vehicles. Many service stations offer towing service, and they are good prospects for employment.

ELECTRICAL SPECIALIST

Most of the work for the electrical specialist is in the area of the battery, alternator, voltage regulator, and starter service and repair. To do this, the specialist also must be able to handle many other electrical and electronic devices.

Ignition contact points are rapidly becoming a thing of the past. Today's engines are controlled by electronic ignition-control devices. On-board computers are abundant. Sometimes repairs are made by linking the car's computer to the shop's "master computer." Instead of replacing parts, you change programming or recalibrate the on-board computer units. The electrical specialist uses sophisticated equipment to determine the source of malfunction in these systems, be they the sensors, actuators, or the computer-controlling devices themselves. There's an emerging specialty for computer diagnostic technicians.

Additionally, the specialist repairs many electrical accessories like power seats, door locks, convertible tops, radios, instruments, sound systems, and lighting systems. The specialist also is involved in the diagnosis and repair of electric motors such as for windshield wipers, heat and air-conditioner blower motors, and starter motors.

This field requires extensive knowledge of electricity and electronics. The specialist must be able to use diagnostic equipment like ammeters, voltmeters, and ohmeters as well as other specialized diagnostic equipment. He or she must know how to read and interpret wiring diagrams. A strong aptitude for mathematics is necessary.

The number of electrical and electronic devices in the automotive industry is destined to grow. There is always a demand for good electrical specialists.

EXHAUST SPECIALIST

There are plenty of opportunities for good exhaust specialists. You need only consider all the independent and franchise muffler shops to recognize the growth in this field.

Exhaust specialists use basic hand tools to remove worn or defective exhaust pipes and replace them. In addition, they must learn to use an acetylene torch and hydraulic pipe bender to fashion exhaust pipes from instructions or to make some custom pipes for special applications.

Exhaust work is dirty and grimy. However, employment as an exhaust specialist is relatively secure. Most exhaust shops also offer some other services like brake and shock absorber replacement, so you can get additional experience. Advancement opportunities are rather limited. The one logical advancement is to shop manager, or in the case of muffler shop chains, to a regional management position. It is also a good training ground and an easy entry-level position to obtain.

MOTORCYCLE MECHANIC

There are more than five million motorcycles registered in America. Although many motorcycle enthusiasts service their own bikes, many rely on the eleven thousand plus professional motorcycle technicians nationwide.

The professional motorcycle technician must diagnose and repair all the systems. Specialized equipment and tools as well as basic hand tools are used to diagnose, adjust, and repair the bike. Although bike technicians may specialize in some special aspect of the vehicle in larger shops, most have to be able to fix all the systems. Some technicians work on one make of motorcycle while others will repair all makes. The demand for motorcycle technicians is very high at the present.

AIR-CONDITIONING SPECIALIST

The air-conditioning specialist uses gauges and specialized leak-detecting tools to diagnose problems in the system. Often a recharge of refrigerant is all that may be needed. Other common jobs include replacing weak or damaged hoses and lines, replacing compressor seals, or rebuilding the compressor. In addition to basic hand tools, the air-conditioning specialist spends several hundred dollars for special tools and equipment.

Air-conditioning service requires special training. It helps to understand the physics and laws of evaporation, condensation, and latent heat of evaporation. Mathematics is important, since measurements taken must be adjusted for atmospheric pressure adjusted to sea level and the level of humidity of the air.

RADIATOR OR COOLING SYSTEM SPECIALIST

Although one may specialize in only radiator and heater core repair, a growing number of technicians are becoming cooling system specialists who service the entire system. The engine cooling system is complex and plays a vital role in overall vehicle operation as well as emission control. The cooling system functions not only to keep the engine temperature at a specified level, but it also doubles as the heating system for passenger comfort.

The radiator specialist traditionally cleaned and repaired radiators and heater cores by soaking them in a caustic bath and physically rodding them out, which involved passing thin rods through the tubes to remove any buildup of corrosion or sludge. Today's radiator or cooling system specialists find themselves using new techniques and tools to service the system.

The cooling system specialist services the entire cooling system and diagnoses causes of overheating like restrictions in the water jacket of the engine, the cylinder head, or head gasket, or problems such as cracked blocks or defective core hole plugs.

Cooling system service represents a substantial investment in equipment to service all the parts and to repair or rebuild them. However, the cooling system technician may work for a shop that supplies all the necessary large equipment, and the technician may have to supply only basic hand tools.

Although cooling system service does require training, it is usually less than many of the other areas of specialization. Most of the work is done indoors, but one of the greatest health risks is from lead poisoning due to the quantities of solder used for radiator repair. In newer shops, this risk is reduced to a minimum by sophisticated air-purifying systems and safety practices.

TRANSMISSION SPECIALIST

The job of transmission specialist is one of the more visible occupational specialists today. There are numerous independent and franchise shops where this person is employed. He or she also may work at auto dealerships, service stations, and other independent repair shops. About sixty-eight hundred shops nationwide employ nearly thirty thousand people.

Although removing and installing the transmission is a dirty and strenuous job, repairing or rebuilding the internal parts of the automatic transmission is a very clean one. In fact, the rebuilding area or room is kept immaculate, since even bits of dust or lint from a rag can cause the transmission to malfunction. The manual transmission is not as critical, but the work is still relatively clean.

Becoming an automatic transmission specialist requires additional training. One must understand the principles of hydraulics as well as mechanics. Transmission specialists must have numerous special tools to service the units. The investment in special tools can be between $3,500 and $6,500.

The trend toward more front-wheel drive cars demands special tools and training in the operation of these new drivetrains. For the interested person, this new avenue may be just the place to look for getting a job fast and making a good wage. There is a shortage of specialists in this area, so the demand is presently very high.

TUNE-UP OR ENGINE PERFORMANCE SPECIALIST

The tune-up specialist diagnoses the condition of the engine with respect to how well it runs according to fuel economy, performance, and emissions. Traditionally, about every twelve thousand miles he or she would replace the spark plugs, ignition points, and condenser. Then he or she would check and adjust the ignition timing and carburetor.

Although this kind of tune-up is still being done, it has become less and less frequent. In fact, the title of tune-up specialist has given way to engine performance specialist, since this more accurately describes the job.

Today's engine performance technician uses sophisticated diagnostic equipment to evaluate the various systems and subsystems of the engine. Machines costing upwards of $20,000 are commonly the basic tool for the engine performance specialist.

Engines and their related controls have become extremely complex. The points have been replaced with electronic modules and on-board computers. Emission controls are an integral part of the engine.

The engine performance specialist usually begins by checking the battery and charging systems. He or she checks and evaluates exhaust emissions. With the aid of computerized diagnostic devices, the specialist evaluates the functioning of the various engine sensors. The control devices are checked. For example, electronic devices actually control the fuel mixture in the carburetor and adjust it many times every second. No longer can the mixture be set by turning a screw—a computer controls it.

An electronic, digital volt/ohmmeter and various specialized hand tools are an essential part of this specialist's toolbox, Engine repair and diagnosis is highly complex, but for the person who can master the field, the rewards are excellent. Wages and salaries are good and advancement opportunities for well-trained technicians are well above average.

CONSTRUCTION EQUIPMENT TECHNICIAN

Construction equipment is a part of the vast field of automotive service. Construction equipment uses both gasoline and diesel engines and includes such things as power shovels, cranes, scrapers, paving machines, road graders, trench-digging machines, bulldozers, and dredges.

Construction equipment mechanics work on all of these items, and some may specialize in lubrication or in repairing one system, such as the tracks on bulldozers. About 106,000 technicians specialize in mobile heavy equipment repair.

OTHER OPPORTUNITIES

Among the other possibilities to explore under the giant heading of automotive service are automobile tester, golf cart repairer, brake repairer, bus inspector, auto parts remanufacturer, spring repairer, brake drum and disc lathe operator, used car renovator, auto engine and drivetrain testers, instructor, writer, race car pit-crew member, upholstery and convertible-top repairer, windshield and auto glass installer, machinist, and military vehicle technician. Just look around. Anything with an engine needs you.

EMERGING TECHNOLOGY MEANS NEW JOBS

An emerging specialty in automotive repair is that of electronics repair technician. These specialists tackle the electronic control units that run today's cars. Since the 1960s, when electronic ignitions became common, electronics have gained an increasingly important role in cars. The heart of exhaust emissions control is an electronic module that adjusts fuel mix and use. *Motor Service* magazine tracked this development in a 1995 article, thus summing up the influence of this trend: "The world of electronics will forever more be part of your daily service practice." The magazine documented how electronics now control engine performance, brake systems, ignition, transmission, and more. While electronics have changed the way technicians work, the new technology also has opened up new opportunities. *Motor Service* estimated that emissions control repair would become a $1 billion business for repair shops around the country—*if* technicians are trained and ready to do the work required by the strict pollution controls we need to keep our air clean.

CHAPTER 12

TOOLS OF THE TRADE

One of the greatest joys of being an automotive technician is that of owning and using tools. There is something satisfying about having just the right tool for a particular job—and knowing how to use it. A technician's tools are as important as the person's hands and mind. The technician cannot make a living without them.

BUY THE BEST

Anyone who is genuinely sincere about a profession as an automotive technician will buy the best tools he or she can afford. Cheap tools may be fine for the person who makes minor repairs around the house, but the professional technician relies on his or her tools to make a living. The tools will be used many times during the course of a single day and must be able to endure constant use. Poor quality tools are a waste of money.

The tools you buy should be durable, sturdy, well finished, and they should look and feel good in the hand. They may be some of the most expensive tools anyone can buy.

Many companies make excellent tools for the professional technician. If you are interested, you might want to write to some of the tool companies and request a catalog and price list. Some current information can be found at www.etools.org.

A SUBSTANTIAL INVESTMENT

Tools can be a substantial investment. The average mechanic's investment in tools is in the range of $7,500 to $11,000 for the basic assortment and toolbox. Some technicians have up to $27,000 invested in tools that they buy during their career. An apprentice set (more than one hundred pieces) with a five-drawer tool chest cost about $2,400 in 2000. For the entry-level technician, the initial investment in tools is about $3,500 to $5,000. Although that is a lot of money, for the professional technician it is a necessary investment.

Many automobile dealerships have a selection of specialized tools, and some independent repair shops and service stations also may supply special tools. If the individual had to supply them, the figure for his or her tool investment would be astronomical.

A 1995 *Motor Service* Equipment and Tool Institute survey found that most technicians spent between $2,000 and $11,000 on their tools. Your choice of an employer and a specialty will play a key role in how much you'll need to invest in tools: only 12 percent of service station employees "owned more than $11,000 worth of tools," but 36 percent of fleet repair shop technicians spent that much or more, as did 30 percent of independent repair shop techs, and 37 percent of car and truck dealership technicians. In other words, the more advanced technicians tended to spend more. If you bought one manufacturer's fully loaded tool chest today (2001), that set alone would retail for $27,000. That may seem like a fortune, but few technicians buy all their tools at once. Vendors and lenders offer financing plans to spread out payments. Your school may have an arrangement with a local tool dealer and can tell you more about the options available.

Fortunately, most automakers are reducing the number of special tools required to service their vehicles. Very few mechanics or shops could cope with the enormous array of special tools required, and often the wrong tools have been used to do the job. This has resulted in damage to the parts, or worse yet, unsatisfactory repairs. Few mechanics have been willing—or able—to pay for the multitude of costly special tools to service every different make and model of vehicle. One alternative is to invest in aftermarket manuals, which can reduce the need for special tools. These manuals describe correct procedures using common tools, the technical manager at the Equipment and Tool Institute points out.

Those who are interested in servicing larger vehicles like trucks and heavy equipment face even higher tool costs. As a general rule, the larger the tool, the greater the cost. A typical end wrench, like a 9/16-inch used on cars, may cost as little as $3.50 or as much as $27.50; a one-inch wrench may cost from $4.50 to $61.00, depending on brand, quality, and source.

ADDITIONAL INVESTMENTS

Besides the initial tool assortment investment, most technicians can expect to spend money every year to replace lost, broken, or stolen tools. According to the Equipment and Tool Institute, the annual replacement cost may amount to about 6 to 11 percent. In other words, for somebody whose gradual basic investment in tools is $8,000, the replacement cost will be from $480 to $880 annually.

Technicians who wish to specialize in an area such as alignment or transmission should expect to invest another $6,800 for the tools necessary to specialize. It is not at all uncommon for professional technicians to spend about $25 to $60 every week for tools. That is more than he or she will most likely spend for lunch.

Tool loss is a big problem. Tools are occasionally lost because they are left in the vehicle that was serviced. Some tools are "lost" because they were used improperly, and they broke. Although many tool companies warranty their tools, they will not replace tools that are damaged due to misuse.

Tools do not usually disappear because of outright theft, although some less than scrupulous person may walk off with a tool or two. What is more frequent is that the tools wind up in some other mechanic's box. Generally, that person did not intend to take the tools. What commonly happens is that someone borrows a tool to help do a job and absentmindedly puts it in his or her own toolbox when the job is done. The person may not notice it for weeks or months. By then he or she has forgotten that it was borrowed from a coworker, or one of the persons has moved to a different job with another employer.

TOOL SECURITY

The most beneficial thing anyone can do to protect tools is to identify them. There are plenty of fine tools that you can use to scribe some identifier into each of your tools. The best identification is to scribe your social security number on them.

Some tool companies sell shadow boxes. For each and every tool, there is a groove, slot, or other type of location where it, and only it, belongs and fits. If one of the spaces is empty, you immediately know that one of your tools is missing. Shadow boxes are well worth the investment.

TOOL CARE

The first step in tool care is to use the correct tool for the job. Misuse not only can damage the tool but is a safety hazard as well.

Second, keep your tools clean. Dirt, oil, and grease in a tool can change the lines of force during use, causing the tool to break.

Third, keep tools in good repair. Some tools naturally wear with use. Chisels are a good example. The points get dull, and heads will mushroom from repeated blows from a hammer. Keep the points sharpened. Use a file to remove the mushroomed area and restore the bevel to the head.

THE BARE NECESSITIES

There are plenty of package deals that the tool manufacturers offer. For the most part they are excellent bargains. However, the choice of tools is a rather personal thing, and there are some that come with the kit that you may seldom use. In addition, there may be tools that you will rely on much of the time that may not be included in the package. If you cannot afford the full package at the start, you may find yourself in debt to the tool company for a long time.

If you are enrolled in a vocational training school or junior college, tool companies will often offer you a discount. Take advantage of the deals if you are financially able.

If you are on a tight budget, there is no use scrimping too much. After all, this is going to be your livelihood.

The Toolbox

A toolbox is much more than the name implies. In fact, it is more of a cabinet than a box. You may spend several hundred dollars to $2,000 on both a top and bottom box, but the first thing to start with is the top.

The top box usually has several drawers that are shallow enough to hold only a variety of tools of a single type. The top area is usually open when the lid is up and is the popular place to arrange your various sockets and drives as well as extensions. Be sure the top closes over your tools and that the drawers and cover lock securely.

Buy a sturdy box. You will be surprised by the weight when it is full of tools. Look for handles and drawer pulls that are strong and convenient. Be sure there are no sharp edges on any of the sheet metal.

A top box with about eight or nine drawers is usually large enough to start with. Besides, you will be able to add a bottom box or an intermediate box at some later date.

A toolbox is vital for keeping your many tools organized. If you don't like organization and precision, you probably aren't interested in this career anyway. Organize your tools the way it best suits your needs, so you can grab any tool you want instantly.

Security is another reason for a tool chest. Most good chests have good locks. It will be impossible to take your tools home with you at the end of the day, so a safe place for them is imperative.

Screwdrivers

You will need lots of screwdrivers—everything from the tiniest jeweler's screwdrivers up to big ones that may be two- or three-feet long. Be sure to get an assortment of straight screwdrivers.

Buy a good set of Phillips screwdrivers, too. The tips, or blades, should be strong and precise.

Another type of fastener frequently found is known as Torx. The head resembles a six-sided hole with the flats, or sides, curved toward the center. Torx fasteners are often found on headlights and interiors. Get a good set of Torx screwdrivers.

Several tool companies make magnetic screwdrivers in which the bits are interchangeable and spare bits are stored in the handle. Not only do magnetic screwdrivers hold screws, they come in handy to pick up a part that has fallen into a tight spot.

Wrenches

Whenever someone says "wrench," you probably visualize the *end wrench* in your mind.

The other popular wrench is the *box end*. This is a closed rather than open end and is available in either six-point or twelve-point styles.

The third type is called a *combination wrench*. The combination wrench will have an open end on one side and a box on the other.

Although most technicians shun the adjustable crescent wrench, there are times that they come in handy.

Line wrenches are sometimes called flare nut wrenches. They are the only kind to use on fluid line fittings such as fuel lines or brakelines.

Tappet wrenches are usually long and quite a bit thinner than the normal open end wrench. They are indispensable for adjusting valves and helpful for getting into tight places.

Ignition wrenches usually come in a set, although you may be able to find them individually. The ignition wrench is very useful in many tight spots, such as behind the dashboard.

The crowsfoot wrench looks like the end of an open end wrench with the handle cut off. Instead of a handle, there is a square hole where a drive from a 3/8-inch ratchet fits. The crowsfoot wrench will get into places where your hand won't fit. For instance, it can be used for loosening the hold-down bolt on the distributor and the hydraulic fluid line for power steering at the steering gearbox.

Pliers

There are numerous types and styles of pliers. They come in all shapes and sizes from the slip-joints that almost everyone has in the kitchen junk drawer to extremely specialized kinds for use on very limited applications. The beginning technician should have a few basics, though.

Slip-joint pliers are the type everyone recognizes. They should never be used anywhere that a wrench should be used, but they are an asset in many places to hold objects.

Unlike slip-joint pliers, Channel-Lock pliers have a tongue and groove arrangement, so they can accommodate a number of jaw openings. Water-pump pliers look a lot like Channel-Lock pliers, but instead of the tongue-in-groove design, they have the pin-and-multiple-hole arrangement like slip-joints. The Channel-Lock pliers are less likely to change jaw openings during use than the water-pump pliers.

Locking pliers are most commonly known by their registered trade name of *Vise-Grips*. When attached to something, they lock in place and leave your hands free. Locking pliers are a definite asset to have in your toolbox.

Snap-ring pliers are used for removing and installing snap rings, which are often found holding a bearing or seal to some sort of shaft, such as an air-conditioning compressor drive shaft. You will need two different types of snap-ring pliers: one each for servicing snap rings that must be squeezed and another for snap rings that must be spread.

There are numerous types of cutting pliers, but the most popular with automotive technicians is the diagonal, or side-cutters. They are especially useful for cutting wires. Be sure to choose ones that have hardened jaws.

Needle-nose pliers have long, tapered, thin jaws that come to a small point at the tip. They are useful for removing and installing tiny clips like those found on a carburetor where your fingers will not fit. Although the basic, straight needle-nose design is the most popular, you also should consider buying a pair that has angled jaws, which can be very handy when trying to work around some neighboring component or a recessed area.

Automobiles and trucks have numerous electrical circuits, and you will find yourself repairing a lot of wiring problems. The most common are electrical shorts or bad grounds, and you will frequently be expected to splice and repair circuits.

There is one tool that will splice, cut, and strip wires—multipurpose electrician's pliers. You will find that this one single tool will be used for almost all of your automotive electrical service, and you should not be without one.

Ratchets and Sockets

Sockets can be used in almost any application that a box or end wrench is used, but with the ratchet drive, the job can be done in a fraction of the time that a wrench would take.

The ratchet drive handle is usually just referred to as the ratchet. This tool gives you the flexibility to turn a fastener in only one direction without the necessity of lifting the tool off the nut or bolt to reposition it to turn it some more.

There are four basic sizes of ratchet drives: $1/4$-inch, $3/8$-inch, $1/2$-inch, and $3/4$-inch. The automobile technician uses the $3/8$-inch tools most of the time and finds the $1/2$-inch handy for most of the heavier work. The truck mechanic uses the $1/2$-inch set most often but uses the $3/4$-inch drive for the heavy jobs.

The sockets that accompany the ratchet are used in much the same manner that wrenches are used. Although sockets are sold individually, they should be initially purchased in sets. The basic set for the 3/8-inch drive usually ranges from 1/16-inch up to 1-inch.

As a general rule, the more expensive the tool is, the better its quality.

Almost all tool companies offer three types of sockets. Hand sockets are designed for use with hand tools. They should never be used on power tools.

The second category is impact sockets. These sockets are especially designed for use on impact drivers that hammer as they turn. Impact sockets are usually black in color, and the walls of the socket are substantially thicker than those on the hand sockets. Impact sockets may be used on hand tools, of course, but hand sockets may never be used on impact tools.

The final category is power sockets. These are designed for use on power nut runners or multispindle machines often found in production. They are not a necessity for the general automotive technician.

All sockets are available in standard and deep designs. If you cannot afford to buy both sets, it is probably best to start with the deep-well sockets.

Universal Joints

Sometimes you may not be able to get a straight shot at the fastener. This is where the universal joint comes in. It allows you to operate your ratchet drive from an angle while maintaining good contact with the fastener. The universal operates much like your wrist in being able to swivel in a complete circle from an angle.

Many beginning technicians buy one or two universal joints that are inserted between the drive and the socket. However, advanced technicians opt for socket sets that have universals built into them.

Other Accessories

There are a few accessories that you should consider. The first is a set of extensions. These come in various lengths, starting at about 1 1/2 inches up to ones in excess of 3 feet. Extensions allow you to reach into distant tight spots where your hand won't go and to work a little further away from the fastener.

A breaker bar is a drive without a ratcheting mechanism. The handle is usually much longer than that for the ratchet and provides you with extra leverage for removing particularly tenacious fasteners.

A speeder can best be described as a crank. It looks just like the old-fashioned cranks that were used to start the cars. Where space permits, it allows you to run up a fastener very quickly. A speeder is useful on the bolts on the oil pan or automatic transmission pan, for example.

A handle drive is very useful with your 1/4-inch sockets. Looking like a screwdriver handle, it has a square drive end to accept interchangeable sockets. If you have a 1/4-inch handle drive, you probably won't have to buy a set of nut drivers.

SPECIALTY TOOLS

Even if you decide not to specialize in any specific area at first, there are several specialty tools that you will need in your day-to-day service and repair jobs.

Feeler Gauges

There are two general kinds of feeler gauges that you need. The first type is the wire gauge used for gapping spark plugs. The spark plug feeler gauges are a set of calibrated wires of increasing thicknesses. Aside from their most frequent use for gapping the electrodes on spark plugs, these gauges can be used any place where the adjoining parts do not both have flat surfaces.

The second, and most popular as well as useful, set of gauges are flat and about the width of an ice cream stick—although much thinner. These gauges are usually sold as a set with each blade $1/1000$ inch thicker than the next. They are particularly important for setting valve clearances or lash and are useful anywhere the distance between two surfaces must be measured.

A special kind of flat feeler gauge is known as the go-no-go gauge. With the go-no-go gauges you will have gapped the valve lash, for instance, precisely if you can just move the thinner section between the surfaces while the stepped-up portion will not pass between the surfaces. These gauges can be used anywhere flat feeler gauges are needed.

Buy the go-no-go gauges as your first set. If you can find the type that have an angled bend in them about halfway down their length, you will find them handy when you must make measurements in tight quarters.

Brake Tools

For basic drum-brake service, you will need a tool for removing and installing the return springs. Various styles and designs of this tool are available. Most mechanics like the kind that resembles a pair of tongs.

Another tool is needed for removing and installing the hold-down springs. It resembles a screwdriver from the handle to the bottom, except there is a cup-shaped tip rather than a blade. Select a hold-down spring tool that is knurled inside the cup. This will help to hold the spring cap into the tool and prevent slipping when you twist it to set the cap.

Finally, you will need at least three different brake adjusting tools that are often called spoons.

For disc brake service, most of your common hand tools are all that you require. One exception is something to push the piston back down into its bore. Although some specific tools are available for this, a good C-clamp is usually all you will need.

Torque Wrenches

The engineers who work for the automobile manufacturers have a torque, or tightening, specification for every nut and bolt on the vehicle. A click-type torque wrench can be set to the desired specification, and once it is reached the wrench will give a clicking sound.

All torque wrenches should be occasionally tested and adjusted should they lose their calibration.

Hammers

"Don't force it. Just get a bigger hammer." That's a joke, and in fact, most professionals will avoid using a hammer unless it is a last resort. However, there are several places where nothing else will do.

You should have at least one twelve-ounce ball-peen hammer. Use it on chisels and punches. The ball-peen is useful for reforming bolt holes in sheet metal like oil pans and valve corners.

You also should own at least one soft-face hammer. Soft-face hammers will not damage parts like steel ones. The face deforms instead of the part being struck.

Dead-blow hammers have heads that are filled with shot. Since the shot continues the force after the hammer makes contact, rebound is reduced.

For heavy-duty purposes you also should have one big hammer in the two- to three-pound range. Many technicians select one known as the engineer's hammer. One side of this double-faced hammer looks like a conventional sledge hammer. The other face is wedge shaped.

Pullers

The automotive technician encounters many items on the job that do not simply slide off their mating part. This is where the puller is needed. The first one to get is a battery cable terminal puller. This puller prevents damage to the battery case when the cable clamp is seized to the battery terminal.

Gear pullers come in a wide assortment of shapes and sizes. To start, choose one that has the flexibility to be used for a variety of purposes. Pullers of this type come with an assortment of legs and jaws so they can be used to remove a variety of items from bearing races to crankshaft gears to steering wheels.

A slide hammer is another type of puller you may need. Slide hammers often are necessary to remove the rear axles on rear-wheel-drive cars.

Chisels and Punches

Never use a screwdriver as a chisel. Cold chisels are for cutting metal while it is cold. They are extremely hard and are liable to chip when struck with a hammer. Keep them sharp, and if the head begins to mushroom, file a champher onto them.

Punches and drift pins are essential. Punches are necessary to make a dimple in the metal before drilling. Drift pins come in a variety of diameters, and only the correct diameter punch should be used to prevent damage to the component. You should buy a good assortment of punches and at least a couple of chisels to start with.

Electronic Diagnostic Tools

Electronic control units, which are actually minicomputers, now affect all of an automobile's operating systems. From ignition to exhaust, electronic systems are vital, and the technician needs special tools to repair these high-tech machines. Technicians often buy their own diagnostic instruments, at least the often-used, handheld models. Repair shops usually buy the larger diagnostic "master computers" and monitors that their technicians use in the shop.

A technician who wants to be ready for electronic diagnostics now needs at least three specialized tools, says Charles Gorman, technical manager of the Equipment and Tool Institute:

1. a scan tool—the device that processes and displays vehicle data link information.
2. a digital multimeter—a test instrument that measures both AC and DC voltages, resistance, frequency, pulse width, and amperage—all on a digital readout.
3. a graphing multimeter, or digital storage oscilloscope—a meter that captures high-frequency electrical signals via a glitch-capture or record function, allowing the technician to diagnose the problem.

More information is available from the institute at etools.org, where you can check on equipment performance guidelines.

Diagnostic tool costs vary. As a point of reference, a scan tool may cost about $350. Digital and scanning meters range from around $100 up into the thousands of dollars, depending on their sophistication and functions.

TOOL INSURANCE

Consider getting insurance on your tools. Although the shop may have a security system and guard dogs, seldom will it have insurance that will cover the loss of the employee's tools.

Most insurance companies will provide a rider to your homeowner's or tenant's homeowner policy for a small charge. Take advantage of the coverage.

CHAPTER 13

LEARNING THE TRADE

There are many ways to learn a subject. One is to read about it and learn the theory as best you can. The other is to perform the task yourself and learn by doing. Both are good methods, but neither one of them is enough. Although experience is an excellent teacher, doing a task without understanding why makes the worker little more than a robot. In the automotive service business, that person is usually referred to as a parts-changer, because that is all he or she is capable of doing.

The first place for an aspiring automotive technician to start is in high school.

It is a difficult thing to admit, but in the past the automotive curriculum was often considered a catch-all for those who could not, or would not, do well in the academic disciplines. No longer is that the case. If you are seriously interested in the field of automotive repair and service, there is much to learn.

Basic courses in mathematics are vital to make computations for necessary adjustments and repairs to vehicular systems. Courses in grammar and English are important because the job requires that you be able to communicate orally and in writing. There is much reading to do in the service business. Technical manuals and trade journals keep the technician informed of new developments and service techniques. Nobody is expected to know all there is to know about every vehicle ever manufactured. You are, however, expected to know where to find the answers and be able to put that information into practice.

If your school offers blueprint reading, it will be beneficial. Courses in electronics and physics will help you understand the principles of operation and then put them into practice.

Take business courses. There is usually much business math involved unless you choose to work for a big shop where all you will do is repair cars.

In most smaller shops and garages, you may have to write the repair order, diagnose the problem, give the customer an estimate, service the vehicle, and finally compute the bill and collect the payment from the customer. Since some technicians go on to become service advisers and service managers, this is good practice, and the skills and knowledge learned early will be a benefit later. You can join the Automotive Service Association and study at the Automotive Management Institute, Bedford, Texas, (800–272–7467: www.asashop.org) for accredited automotive managers, or get general business training from local schools and colleges.

TAKE TIME AND PLAN

Too many people never get around to planning their careers. They just bounce around from job to job and fall into a career by default. Since most people will spend the better part of their lives working—from twenty-five to forty-five years—it is well worth your time and effort to make some career planning decisions.

The first rule is simple: take the time and plan. Even a few days or weeks in planning is a lot better than a lifetime of regret or underemployment. What is underemployment? That is what happens to someone who has the ability and aptitude for getting a better job, but since he or she is not sufficiently trained, he or she ends up in jobs that do not offer enough challenge, money, or personal satisfaction. They know they can do better, but they aren't able to land that job for lack of either experience or training.

Planning a career takes thought. It also takes enough information to make a good decision. It is surprising how even a few hours of investigation can pay off big dividends for your future. Since you are reading this book, you are taking one of the first steps.

As you are probably aware, jobs are becoming increasingly specialized. In fact, the U.S. Department of Labor lists more than twenty-thousand career specialties in its *Dictionary of Occupational Titles*. In addition, new technology is creating a demand for a much more highly skilled work force, and employers are putting a premium on persons who have those specific skills that are beneficial to their operation. The automotive field is becoming more specialized every year. Automotive systems are each growing more complex as the auto manufacturers find new ways to increase fuel economy and to reduce emissions. According to estimates from the Department of Labor, most of the future jobs will require some sort of specialized technical or trade school training, if not college.

POINTS IN PERSONAL PLANNING

The first things to consider in planning your personal future are your interests. Take the time to list all the things you like to do. Are you happy working indoors or outdoors? Do you like working with people, or do you prefer to work alone? Would you like to wear a necktie or business suit, or do you want to wear jeans to work? Consider all the things you enjoy doing and list them. If it is hard to do, consider some of the things you have done in the past, and then pick out the common facets that have made them pleasurable. You soon will see a pattern emerge and learn what you like to do.

The next item to consider is salary or wages. What is the starting salary of the field you choose? What can you expect to be earning in a couple of years on the job? How about ten or fifteen years down the road? Although we have tried to indicate what kind of money you may expect to earn in this book, there is no better way to find out than to go and ask someone who is employed in the trade. You also may get some help from your local state employment office.

While you are at it, check into the job conditions. Visit a few repair facilities and see firsthand what the shop is like. Would you like to work in the kind of environment you see? Now is the time to make sure that a career in automotive service is everything you expect it to be. Make the right choice today, one you'll be happy with the rest of your life.

Investigate the demand for the type of job you choose from the vast array offered under the umbrella called automotive service. Is the demand greater than the number of persons qualified to fill those jobs? If so, you've chosen something that will almost guarantee you employment. For example, there is usually a bigger demand for men and women who are expert in air-conditioning service in the hotter areas of the country than in the colder north. Fortunately, automotive service will continue to be in demand.

Another thing to consider is mobility. Would you like to work in your present locale, or would you prefer to move somewhere else? With automotive service, you can just about pick where you want to work. At present there are job openings almost everywhere in the country, but there are fewer jobs available in the industrialized areas of the east and midwest. The openings do exist; there are just fewer of them.

Finally, find out what the educational requirements are of the job in which you are interested. You must know your trade well to make yourself marketable. You can prove your worth with experience, certification, or a diploma from a reputable trade school or junior college. You may learn enough in a trade school to land some jobs in as little as a few months. To earn an associate degree from a junior or community college, it usually takes two years. In automotive service, a bachelor's degree from college usually won't do you as much good as technical training from a trade school or community college. However, some of the most skilled technicians have college degrees in addition to their trade school training. All techs, no matter how advanced, continue to attend workshops and seminars to update their skills. In the automotive trades, learning is a lifelong process, according to Bill Boyd, National Technical Training Manager for Daimler Chrysler.

In 1984 the National Institute for Automotive Service Excellence (ASE) set up the National Automotive Technicians Education Foundation (NATEF). Both secondary (high school) and postsecondary (college) programs are certified by the NATEF at the school's request. The areas in which a school can be certified are the same ones in which a technician can get certified by the National Institute for Automotive Service Excellence. These include engine repair, automatic transmission/transaxle, manual drivetrain and axles, front-end, brakes, electrical systems, heating and air-conditioning, and engine performance.

New schools are being certified all the time. Although some of the schools certified at the time this book was published are listed in Appendix D, you may write to find any other schools added more recently. Check the ASE websites www.asecert.org or www.natef.org. Or mail your request for information to:

NATEF
13505 Dulles Technology Drive
Herndon, VA 20171-3421

TRADE AND TECHNICAL SCHOOLS

Trade and technical schools are private schools that specialize in career training. They are usually small, single-purpose schools that specialize in preparing a person to move right into the work world upon graduation. You won't find courses in the humanities or history in a trade school, but you will learn much about your chosen field within a minimum of time.

Since you need not take extraneous subjects, you save time because only classes in your trade are taught. There are no extracurricular activities like a football team, only important subjects relevant to your career. Although the tuition may range from hundreds to thousands of dollars, you will finish a lot sooner than if you choose to go to college.

You generally need a high school diploma or general equivalency diploma (GED) to enter, but some schools will waive these requirements if you have plenty of work experience. Schools approved by the Career College Association do not discriminate in their admission policies, and many minority students will find avenues open that may have been previously closed to them. Other accrediting agencies and your state education department, as well as organizations like the American Association of Community Colleges, also can help.

Usually the classes are small and friends are easily made. The small class size is helpful, because the instructor can devote more time and individual attention to each student.

Most of the schools also offer job placement assistance. Placement is an important part of their program because these schools are basically a private business. They strive for high success in placement. If they are good at getting jobs for their graduates, more students will be encouraged to enter, and the business thrives. Vocational schools work closely with potential employers, and over the years they have usually developed many good contacts who are anxious to have well-trained and qualified people working in their places of business.

Some schools provide other placement aids, such as resume writing and interviewing techniques that can help you land a job and even change jobs in the future. Check with the school for these services before you choose it.

HOW TO CHOOSE A SCHOOL

The first step in choosing a trade or technical school is to write to a few and request their catalogs. There is a partial list of trade schools that offer automotive service training in Appendix D at the end of this book. Once you receive their catalogs, compare them for the courses you want and also compare them according to the following checklist:

1. *State licensing.* Is the school licensed by your state's postsecondary licensing bureau? If there is no mention in the catalog, check with your state's department of education. Although a few states do not require licensing, most of them do.
2. *Accreditation.* The U.S. Department of Education has guidelines that it follows in issuing an accrediting agency the right to accredit schools.

The agency examines the school, and the school must meet the agency's standards for education quality, teaching ability, and administrative integrity. The school's accreditation is usually listed in the school's catalog, but it is a good idea to double-check by contacting the accrediting agency itself. The National Institute for Automotive Service Excellence also accredits schools.

3. *Courses.* Check to see if the courses offered are up to date, well rounded, and of high quality. Find out who teaches them. Is the instructor someone with professional experience in automotive service? Find out how many and what kinds of courses are necessary for graduation and how long it will take. Also ask if they offer certificates, associate's degrees, or both.

4. *Equipment and facilities.* Find out what kind of classrooms, buildings, and facilities the school offers. Are they modern? See that the equipment they use is up-to-date and is reflective of the kinds of equipment in use in actual repair shops and garages.

5. *Hands-on training.* See if the school has a shop setup that duplicates those found in the real world. With a trade like automotive repair and service, it is vital that you get plenty of hands-on experience.

6. *Placement assistance.* Does the school offer placement assistance to all the students? How long will it keep trying on your behalf to help you land a job? Check to see if it will help you after you graduate. Ask for a list of students that it has helped place and contact them. See if the graduates are satisfied with their jobs. Find out what kinds of jobs they have landed.

7. *Cost.* The big question is how much is it going to cost? Get the total cost for everything, including tuition, books, tools, and lab fees. Ask yourself if you can realistically afford the school. Inquire as to whether the school offers tuition assistance or can help you find a part-time job to help you pay for your education. Ask about the school's refund policy.

Of course, the best way to find out about the school is to visit it in person. Visit with the staff and faculty. Ask to observe some of the classes in session. During breaks, talk with some of the other students and get their honest impressions of the school. Find out if they are happy. Check out the buildings and equipment. Make sure they are as the catalog described them. Again, ask for a list of recent graduates. Take the time and effort to contact some of them. Find out if they think the school helped them get their jobs.

FREE INFORMATION

Start with the U.S. Department of Education (www.ed.gov), which has compiled a huge database of schools and colleges (see Appendix D.)

The Accrediting Commission of Career Schools and Colleges of Technology, an independent agency, is one of the largest and most respected accrediting agencies in America. It has several publications that are available to you at no charge.

Ask your college counselor about accredited schools, or write to the commission to request information, such as the annual *Directory of Private Career Schools and Colleges of Technology*. Write to:

> Accrediting Commission of Career Schools and Colleges of Technology
> 2101 Wilson Boulevard, Suite 302
> Arlington, VA 22201
> 703–247–4212

The commission emphasizes that a student should compare all the schools in his or her area that offer the desired program. Get school catalogs, talk to counselors, and ask about teachers, fees, and job placement possibilities.

See Appendix D for a list of accredited auto technician schools.

TYPICAL COURSE DESCRIPTIONS

When you contact a trade or technical school you will receive a catalog. Carefully read the course descriptions to determine if the school offers the subjects and covers the areas you are interested in learning about. Here are some typical skills you'll acquire at the schools that offer the AYES program (Automotive Youth Education Systems), a school-to-work program that begins in high school and continues through a post–high school program in cooperation with several car manufacturers and their dealerships, at colleges around the country.[1]

Technical Skills

Engine Repair

- general engine diagnosis, removal and reinstallation
- cylinder head and valve train diagnosis and repair

---

[1]Source: Automotive Youth Education Systems, AYES, Inc., Detroit, MI.

- engine block diagnosis and repair
- lubrication and cooling systems diagnosis and repair

Automatic Transmission/Transaxle

- general transmission and transaxle diagnosis
- transmission and transaxle maintenance and adjustment
- in-vehicle transmission and transaxle repair
- off-vehicle transmission and transaxle repair

Manual Drivetrain/Axle

- clutch diagnosis and repair
- transmission diagnosis and repair
- transaxle diagnosis and repair
- drive and half-shaft universal and CV joint diagnosis and repair
- rear axle diagnosis and repair
- four-wheel-drive/all-wheel-drive component diagnosis and repair

Suspension/Steering

- steering and suspension systems diagnosis and repair
- wheel alignment diagnosis, adjustment, and repair
- wheel and tire diagnosis and repair

Brakes

- hydraulic systems diagnosis and repair
- drum brake diagnosis and repair
- disk brake diagnosis and repair
- power assist units diagnosis and repair
- miscellaneous (wheel bearings, parking brakes, electrical, etc.) diagnosis and repair
- anti-lock brake systems

Electrical/Electronic Systems

- general electrical system diagnosis
- battery diagnosis and service
- starting system diagnosis and repair
- charging system diagnosis and repair
- lighting system diagnosis and repair
- gauges, warning devices, driver information systems diagnosis and repair

- horn and wiper/washer diagnosis and repair
- accessories diagnosis and repair

Heating/Air Conditioning

- a/c system diagnosis and repair
- refrigeration system component diagnosis and repair
- heating and engine cooling systems diagnosis and repair
- operating systems and related controls diagnosis and repair
- refrigerant recovery, recycling, and handling

Engine Performance

- general engine diagnosis
- computerized engine controls diagnosis and repair
- ignition systems diagnosis and repair
- fuel, air induction, and exhaust systems diagnosis and repair
- emissions control systems diagnosis and repair
- engine-related services

Employability Skills

- effective self-motivation techniques
- time management skills
- stress management skills
- communication skills
- interpersonal skills
- presentation of a favorable, businesslike image
- team participation skills
- standard business/social etiquette
- ability to develop a resume and an employment portfolio
- ability to complete a job application successfully and interview for a job

As you can see from the skill descriptions, it should be a simple matter to determine if a school offers the skills that you require. The courses are not the same from school to school, and you should take the time to select the one that most closely fits your expectations and objectives.

Automotive Youth Education Systems
2701 Troy Center Drive, Suite 450
Troy, MI 48084
www.ayes.com

COSTS OF SCHOOLING

Of course, cost will be a major factor in deciding which trade or technical school to enroll in. Keep in mind that you are making an investment in your future and that money spent today can pay off in the future by helping you to land a higher paying job.

When requesting a catalog from a school, also ask for a schedule of fees for the course or courses in which you are interested. For example, costs at Prairie State College are $60 per credit hour. An A.A.S. degree program requires 45 hours; General Education requirements add 15 hours. Tuition for district residents is $3,600 a year. Other costs may include books, lab fees, out-of-district resident costs, and so on.

COMMUNITY AND JUNIOR COLLEGES

A prime source of advanced training in the automotive technology field is the community or junior college. One of the greatest advantages of community or junior colleges is that they often offer full-time day classes as well as evening and, occasionally, Saturday classes. For the person who cannot afford to go to school full-time, this can be a lifesaver. The student can pursue a full-time job and get an education during evenings and weekends. Many of the schools also offer intensive summer programs that enable the student to complete about a half of a semester of work in as little as eight or ten weeks.

ADMISSIONS

Most community colleges have an open-door policy, but preference is given to those who reside in the community that a particular college services. Out-of-district students do have an opportunity to enter the school, however, and should consult with the college itself or their high school guidance counselor.

Usually students seeking admission must supply grade transcripts from high school or verification of passing the GED tests. American College Test (ACT) scores are sometimes also requested. These scores are usually used for guidance and counseling and to help determine admission to some programs. Some colleges may require additional testing.

In general, the normal class load is from 12 to 17 credit hours. Anyone taking fewer than 12 hours is usually considered a part-time student. Part-time students may take as little as one credit hour at many schools. A credit hour usually represents one 50-minute period of classwork per week or the equivalent in laboratories or other types of activities.

TUITION AND FEES

All colleges have set tuition prices that they charge their local students, and those from outside the community usually have to pay an additional premium. The best thing to do is contact the college or colleges of your choice and find out what the charges are. You may be expected to prove your residency. Other fees usually include an activity fee, application fees, graduation fees, and laboratory fees.

To help students meet their financial obligations, many schools have assistance programs that help the student find part-time or even full-time employment. You should check with the school's placement officer for assistance. If you can prove the need, you may be eligible for a grant such as a Basic Educational Opportunity Grant (BEOG) or perhaps a local state monetary award or grant. The college also may be able to help you get a loan that is guaranteed by the state or federal government. Some students may be able to take advantage of Veterans Administration (VA) benefits if they are veterans of the armed forces. If you think you may qualify for social security benefits or state vocational rehabilitation money, be sure to check into these possibilities.

If you need financial assistance, the best thing to do is contact the college and ask for help in applying for such assistance. The people there are usually more than happy to help you.

CERTIFICATES AND DEGREES

Most community colleges offer a two-year associate degree or one-year certificate for automotive service. Here are some of the courses required to obtain a certificate in automotive services from a community college, Prairie State College in Chicago Heights, Illinois.

AUTO 101-01   Basic Automobile Service and Systems   Credits: 3.00
Introduces automotive systems and service. Includes safety systems, drive lines, engines, transmissions, transaxles, and more. $35 lab fee.

AUTO 102-01   Automotive Engines   Credits: 3.00
Prerequisite AUTO 101 or equivalent; 3 credit hours. Focuses on automotive engine repair, disassembly, adjustments, assembly, and operation. Service units include block, cylinder heads, valve assembly, lubrication system, and cooling system. $35 lab fee.

AUTO 112-BH   Sheet Metal Repairs–Body Adjustments   Credits: 4.00
Prerequisite AUTO 111 or concurrent registration; 4 credit hours. Metal and fiberglass panel repairs, reshaping, sectioning, clipping, and replacement operations are performed on the hood, deck, door, frame, and door jamb. $50 lab fee.

AUTO 202-01   Automotive Brake Systems   Credits: 3.00
Prerequisite AUTO 101 or equivalent; 3 credit hours. Component repair operations, adjustments, and performance testing of drum and disk brake systems. Introduction to computer systems that control the brake system. $35 lab fee.

AUTO 202-02   Automotive Brake Systems   Credits: 3.00
Prerequisite AUTO 101 or equivalent; 3 credit hours. Component repair operations, adjustments, and performance testing of drum and disk brake systems. Introduction to computer systems that control the brake system. $35 lab fee.

AUTO 206-01   Automotive Engine Performance   Credits: 3.00
Prerequisite AUTO 101, 102, 107, 211; 3 credit hours. This course covers diagnosing and repairing complex engine and computer problems and driveability problems of the modern automobile. $35 lab fee.

AUTO 207-01   Automotive Heating/Air-Conditioning   Credits: 3.00
Prerequisite AUTO 101, 107; 3 credit hours. Component repair operations, adjustments, and performance testing are performed on heating, defrosting, and air-conditioning systems. $35 lab fee.

AUTO 208-01   Automatic Transmissions/Transaxles   Credits: 3.00
Prerequisite AUTO 101, 205; 3 credit hours. Component repair operations, adjustments, and performance testing on automatic transmissions, transmission controls, and auto transaxle transmissions. $35 lab fee.

AUTO 210-01　　**Automotive Electricity/Electronics II**　　**Credits: 3.00**
Prerequisite AUTO 101, 107; APPIE 101; 3 credit hours. Electrical circuit identification, isolation, testing, repair, and component operation. $35 lab fee.

AUTO 211-01　　**Automotive Computer Systems**　　**Credits: 3.00**
Prerequisite AUTO 101, 107, 210; APPIE 101; 3 credit hours. Cover operational aspects of automotive computer output/input control systems, performance diagnosis procedures, and repair. $35 lab fee.

AUTO 223-MC　　**Automotive Parts Management**　　**Credits: 2.00**
Training includes use of parts, equipment, supply catalogs, pricing procedures, and more.

AUTO 299-01　　**Internship Automotive**　　**Credits: 2.00**
Prerequisite 12 hours in AUTO and consent of coordinator; 2 credit hours. This course provides on-the-job experience combined with supervision. It is designed to present the service technician with a performance view of the automotive body service profession.

To get a certificate from a community college, you need to do a lot of work and learning. The time and money spent in training is well worth it, though.

Another school, Triton College, River Grove, Illinois, offers a choice of programs: An associate's degree takes a little longer but enhances the technical education with courses in the humanities and sciences. An auto technician certificate program is strictly devoted to auto repair. There are also several sub-specialty certificates, such as engine performance and brake systems.

Automotive Technology Degree
Associate Applied Science Degree

Semester One		Credit Hours
AUT 112	Introduction to Automotive Technology	3
AUT 114	Fuel Management Systems	4
AUT 127	Automotive Electricity & Electronics	4
RHT 124	Communications 1 or	
RHT 101	Freshman Rhetoric & Comp 1	3
TEC 122	Elementary Technical Mathematics 2	3
Total		**17**

Semester Two		Credit Hours
AUT 129	Automotive Electricity & Electronics	3
AUT 136	Brake, Hardware, & Chassis Repair	4
AUT 150	Auto Power-Plant Overhaul &	
	Rebuilding	5
HUM 126	Humanities	1
RHT 138	Communications II or	
RHT 102	Freshman Rhetoric & Comp II or	
SPE 101	Principles of Effective Speaking	3
Total		**16**

Semester Three		Credit Hours
AUT 226	Engine Performance & Diagnosis	5
AUT 240	Steering, Suspension, & Alignment	4
AUT 275	Transmission & Drive Systems	5
HTH 104	Science or Personal Health or	
HTH 281	First Aid & CPR	2
Total		**16**

Semester Four		Credit Hours
AUT 230	Computerized Engine Controls or	
AUT 277	Advanced Automatic Transmission Repair	5
AUT 280	Automotive Heating &	
	Air-Conditioning Fundamentals	2
AUT 282	Advanced Automotive Heating &	
	Air-Conditioning	2
CIS 151	Introduction to Microcomputers	1
SSC 190	Contemporary Society or	
PSC 150	American Government:	
	Organization & Powers or	
HIS 151	History of the U.S. to 1865	3
ENT 105	Industrial Physics (2)	3
Total		**16**

| **Total credits required for graduation** | | **65** |

Automotive Technology Certificate

Semester One		Credit Hours
AUT 112	Introduction to Automotive Technology	3
AUT 114	Fuel Management Systems	4
AUT 127	Automotive Electricity & Electronics	4
AUT 280	Automotive Heating & Air-Conditioning Fundamentals	2
Total		**13**

Semester Two		Credit Hours
AUT 129	Automotive Electricity & Electronics	3
AUT 136	Brake, Hardware, & Chassis Repair	4
AUT 150	Auto Power-Plant Overhaul & Rebuilding	5
AUT 226	Engine Performance & Diagnosis	5
Total		**17**

Semester Three		Credit Hours
AUT 240	Steering, Suspension, & Alignment	4
AUT 275	Transmission & Drive Systems	5
AUT 282	Advanced Heating and Air-Conditioning	2
AUT 227	Advanced Automatic Transmission Repair or	
AUT 230	Computerized Engine Controls	5
Total		**16**
Total credits required		**46**

Automotive Brake and Suspension Certificate

Semester One		Credit Hours
AUT 112	Introduction to Automotive Technology	3
AUT 127	Automotive Electricity & Electronics	4
Total		**7**

Semester Two		Credit Hours
AUT 136	Brake, Hardware, & Chassis Repair	4
AUT 240	Steering, Suspension, & Alignment	4
Total		**8**

Total credits required		**15**

Automotive Engine Performance Certificate

Semester One		Credit Hours
AUT 112	Introduction to Automotive Technology	3
AUT 114	Fuel Management Systems	4
AUT 127	Automotive Electricity & Electronics	4
Total		**11**

Semester Two		Credit Hours
AUT 129	Electricity & Electronics II	3
AUT 226	Engine Performance & Diagnostics	5
Total		**8**

Semester Three		Credit Hours
AUT 230	Computerized Engine Controls	5

Total credits required		**24**

Automotive Engine Repair Certificate

Semester One		Credit Hours
AUT 112	Introduction to Automotive Technology	3
AUT 114	Fuel Management Systems	4
Total		**7**

Semester Two		Credit Hours
AUT 127	Electricity & Electronics I	4
AUT 150	Power-Plant Overhaul & Rebuilding	5
Total		**9**

Total credits required		**16**

Automotive Transmission Certificate

Semester One		Credit Hours
AUT 112	Introduction to Automotive Technology	3
AUT 127	Automotive Electricity & Electronics	4
Total		**7**

Semester Two		Credit Hours
AUT 136	Brake, Hardware, & Chassis Repair	4
AUT 275	Transmission & Drive Systems	5
Total		**9**

Semester Three		Credit Hours
AUT 227	Advanced Automatic Transmission Repair	5
Total credits required		**21**

AUTO COMPANIES' TRAINING SCHOOLS

Almost all of the automobile manufacturing companies provide advanced training for the technicians who work in their dealerships. The main catch, however, is that you usually have to be employed by a dealership or have dealership sponsoring to enter one of these programs. Remember, too, that you may be studying only the manufacturer's cars. The best place to find out more about dealer-sponsored training is to contact some dealers in your area.

General Motors—Automotive Service Educational Program

In the spring of 1981, General Motors started an innovative program of education that opened new doors for those interested in automotive technical training. General Motors calls it ASEP, which is an acronym for Automotive Service Educational Program. It is a two-year training program that is offered through community colleges and GM dealerships. It features a blend of classroom training mixed with on-the-job experience. Today sixty-five colleges in the United States and sixteen colleges in Canada are affiliated.

One of the schools involved in the cooperative program is Triton College in River Grove, Illinois, a suburb of Chicago. Triton's program is typical of those offered at other community colleges across the nation. The school works closely with the auto manufacturers to keep its curriculum up to date. One example is Triton's GM affiliation. (Note: Triton also works with other car manufacturers and models.)

Basically the GM Automotive Service Educational Program (ASEP) is designed to upgrade the technical competence and professional level of the incoming dealership technician. The curriculum is designed by General Motors, in cooperation with the college, and it does provide for a two-year associate degree in automotive service technology. The student must go to school and work at one of the dealerships. For example, the student may spend the first 11 weeks at the college and follows that up with 8 weeks at the dealership in the first semester. The student then goes back to school for another 11 weeks followed by 8 more weeks in the dealership, and so on. The work at the dealership is supposed to parallel as closely as possible what the student learned in class.

Since considerable time is spent at the dealership, it is a requirement of the program that the student have the sponsoring of a General Motors dealer. If you can't find a sponsoring dealer, you can write directly to the General Motors. Address your request to the ASEP General Motors Service Technology Group, 1650 Research Drive, Suite 200, Troy, MI 48083. In addition to the instructional program, students also may work part-time at the dealership to help pay for their tuition, but it is not necessary.

Tuition will vary from school to school, usually ranging between $3,000 to $5,000 a year, for students who live in-district. You'll have to add the necessary books for the entire program. Those living outside the district must pay an additional premium. You may be able to secure an out-of-district authorization from your home community college to get the in-district rate. Contact the admissions officer at your local community college.

In addition to the tuition and books, the student will be expected to buy the necessary hand tools, which will probably run about $600 to begin with and an additional $250 in tools as you go along.

Although at present the program is limited to those who can obtain dealership sponsorship, it is highly possible that the training may be offered to the aspiring technician at large, so it would be a good idea to contact your community college and find out.

The following car manufacturers, among others, might be able to supply you with additional information in the form of brochures, booklets, and other materials. Since they all offer training programs, they will be glad to explain their programs and how you can enroll.

Chrysler Apprenticeship Program (CAP)
DaimlerChrysler Motors Corp.
Dealer Technical Operations
CAP Program
2367 Walton Boulevard
CIMS 428-00-00
Auburn Hills, MI 48326-1955
www.cap.daimlerchrysler.com

Ford Motor Company Automotive Student Service Educational Training
(ASSET)
Ford Parts and Service Division
www.fordasset.com

Automotive Service Educational Program (ASEP)
General Motors ASEP
1650 Research Drive, Suite 200
Troy, MI 48083
www.gmste.com

Professional Automotive Career Training (PACT)
Honda Industrial Education Liaison
American Honda Motor Co.
1919 Torrance Boulevard
Mail Stop 500-2C-11B
Torrance, CA 90501

Professional Cooperative Apprenticeship Program
(PROCAP)
Nissan PROCAP
P.O. Box 191
Gardena, CA 90248

Toyota Technical Education Network (T-TEN)
Toyota Motor Sales, USA, Inc.
19001 South Western Avenue
Torrance, CA 90509

INTERNSHIP

There is yet another way for the "green" person to break into the field of automotive technician. Say that you are looking for a job and all the employers you meet want only someone with experience or training. The obvious question you might well ask is, "If they only hire people with experience, how can I get experience unless someone hires me?" It is a vicious circle. One way to break that circle is with an internship.

For a minimum wage, or perhaps no wage at all, you may be able to get a job at a local service station or independent repair shop. You may have to accept menial jobs until you can demonstrate that you are capable of more responsible work. But remember, you are making an investment in your future. You may even discover that the occupation is not for you. This way you've spent nothing but some time, and you've learned an important lesson.

Ask your counselor for books on the subject.

APPRENTICESHIP PROGRAMS

Apprenticeships once were the only way to enter the automotive trades. However, the opportunities for apprenticeships have lessened in recent years. More often, career-related education in high school and a community college—plus good grades—will win you the chance to work with a dealership or an independent shop that may sponsor you while you complete your education. If you do have the opportunity for a true apprenticeship under a master technician—take it! The experience will be well worth your time. Some efforts are under way to revive the apprenticeship system, based on the very successful European model, and bring the same pride of craftmanship and guild spirit to American automotive shops. The traditional apprenticeship path is described here, and it will give you an idea of what you'll need to study, no matter what auto technician program you attend.

Apprenticeship programs are designed to teach a particular trade by placing a person in a job and exposing him or her to all facets of that trade during instruction. Along with on-the-job training, there are required amounts of instruction in theory. Formal instruction classes are held at local schools or community colleges. Sometimes the training is offered at the person's place of employment. Occasionally correspondence courses are necessary.

More advanced aspects of the job are taught to the apprentice as he or she becomes proficient in the various basic skills. The programs usually take from two to four years to complete. Once the person has finished his or her apprenticeship term, he or she should be a highly skilled and valued employee.

The United States Department of Labor Bureau of Apprenticeship and Training, in cooperation with the Automotive Service Councils, developed a national apprenticeship program in 1977.

In a letter to the United States Department of Labor, George W. Merwin, III, the executive vice president of the Automotive Service Councils, said, "Our current energy crisis and rising standards of pollution control deem it absolutely necessary that any individual charged with the responsibility of servicing or repairing a motor vehicle must be a professional. The individual must have received the best possible training before being given the responsibility of preparing a vehicle which will go out onto the streets and become an integral part of our environment. How the car, truck, or bus is serviced will have a great bearing on the outcome of current economic and environmental problems, and more importantly, the safety of the driver and passengers."

Entering an Apprenticeship Program

If you are interested in an apprenticeship program, the first step is to contact an employer in the field in which you are interested. It you are unsure of which employers are involved, contact the local labor union that represents workers in the field. Another good place to start is with the state employment service office in your area.

All apprentices have an obligation to ensure their own success by applying themselves diligently in the shop, doing good work, and learning their trade. It is their responsibility to preserve their self-respect and maintain the respect of those with whom they work, their employer, and the customers they serve. They must make every effort to understand the apprenticeship program and abide by all the rules and regulations established by the apprenticeship committee. Apprentices also learn about business ethics.

They are expected to purchase their own textbooks and any other needed items, although some employers pay for all or part of the cost of tools and textbooks, which will become the student's personal property and a start at compiling tools and books for their professional use.

Apprentices need to submit all reports required by the apprenticeship committee and meet with the committee when instructed to do so. On their own initiative, they are expected to attend classes or complete home study assignments made by the apprenticeship committees or their instructors. Time spent in such study is not considered as hours of work, and they will receive no pay for time so spent unless they are required to perform such study during their regular hours of work.

Qualifications for Apprenticeship

To be eligible for apprenticeship, applicants must be at least eighteen years old. They have to be physically fit for the work of the trade and must have a doctor's certificate of health. The employer will pay for the examination.

Applicants accepted for an apprenticeship program who have been employed in the trade may be granted advanced standing as apprentices. Of course, the committee will check the work history and require such applicants to take an examination that covers practical experience and related instruction subjects.

Applicants who are admitted to the advanced standing will be paid the wage rate of the period in which they are placed.

An apprentice who claims previous experience will be expected to furnish evidence of previous employment by a letter from any businesses where be or she was employed, detailing the dates of employment and the type of work performed. The person also will be required to supply a record of previous related instruction subjects and work experience.

Apprenticeship Agreement

Each apprentice and the employer will sign an agreement, and copies will be given to the apprentice, the apprenticeship committee, and the registration agency. The apprenticeship standards, signed by the employer, contain a description of the trade to be learned, a schedule of the work processes and wage rates, and a requirement that the apprentice shall attend related instruction on theory for the time required to learn the trade.

The employer is expected to make every effort to provide reasonably continuous employment for apprentices.

Apprentices usually have to serve a probationary period of at least five hundred hours of reasonably continuous employment. During this time the committee may terminate or cancel the agreement, upon receiving a letter from the employer or the apprentice, without the formality of a hearing. However, after the five-hundred-hour probationary period, the agreement cannot be cancelled without the opportunity for a hearing by the committee.

Responsibilities of Apprentices

When applicants sign the apprenticeship agreement, they voluntarily agree to abide by the provisions of the apprenticeship program. Here are some of the responsibilities and obligations imposed on apprentices during the apprenticeship program:

- To perform diligently and faithfully the work of the trade and duties assigned by the employer, supervisor, or journeyman, in accordance with the provisions of the local program.
- To respect the property of the customer, employer, journeyman, and others and to abide by the working rules and regulations of the employer and the committee.
- To attend regularly and complete satisfactorily the required hours of instruction in subjects related to the trade.
- To maintain records of work experience and related instruction as may be required by the committee.
- To develop safe working habits and conduct themselves in their work in such a manner as to ensure their own safety as well as that of their fellow workers.
- To work for the person to whom they are assigned.
- To conduct themselves at all times in a creditable, ethical, and moral manner, realizing that much time, money, and effort are being spent in affording them an opportunity to become competent technicians.
- To be neat in appearance at all times.
- To furnish the required hand tools necessary to perform the work of an apprentice.
- To purchase their own textbooks or any other items that will become their own property. Some employers agree to purchase textbooks for students who maintain an acceptable grade average.

Related Instruction

As a part of the apprenticeship program, apprentices are required to complement their on-the-job training with formal instruction. Apprentices enroll in and attend related instruction classes for a set number of hours stipulated for the trade they are learning. A minimum of 144 hours of related instruction each year of the apprenticeship is normally considered necessary. Apprentices are expected to exercise the same diligence in their studies as they do in their work on the job.

Examination

The regular period for advancement is after one thousand hours. The committee, however, may require apprentices to appear before it and present their work progress records. The examinations will cover both the on-the-job and related instructional subjects. Apprentices may be required to repeat a certain process if they cannot prove during the examination that the subject is fully understood. If they show that they do not have the ability to become competent craft workers, their apprenticeship agreements may be terminated.

Responsibilities of Employers

The apprentice is not the only one who has obligations to the program. The employer is an integral part and has some responsibilities, too. The employer's duties were developed by the Automotive Service Association in its former apprentice program (now inactive). Similar duties are incorporated into some of the new school-to-work programs being developed by auto manufacturers. For example, each employer designates a journeyman or supervisor to act as the supervisor of apprentices on the job and be responsible for seeing that every apprentice is given the variety of work experience on the job required to make them skilled in all aspects of their trade.

Hours of Employment

The workday and workweek for an apprentice is the same as for the journeyman, and he or she is subject to the same conditions. The employer is not allowed to have overtime or out-of-town work interfere with the apprentice's related instruction in the theory part of the learning program. The apprentice is not allowed to work alone. He or she must work under the supervision of the employer, supervisor, or designated journeyman at all times. The apprentice is not allowed to work overtime without being under the direction of an immediate supervisor or journeyman.

Certification of Completion

Upon completing the entire apprenticeship program, the apprentice will be awarded a certificate of completion from the appropriate registration agency, either federal or state.

SAMPLE WORK PROCESSES

The following is the recommended program that the Automotive Service Councils suggested in years past. It is still a good model for apprenticeships. Not all programs will be the same, but all of the essential items on this list should be a part of the apprentice's obligations before being awarded his or her certificate and being advanced to journeyman technician. These recommendations for a four-year apprenticeship are a guide that should be followed as closely as conditions permit:

Automobile Technician

Recommended Work-Experience Schedule	*Approximate Hours*
a. Shop routine (new vehicle service, body service, installing accessories, and keeping shop clean and orderly)	500
b. Brakes (adjusting, relining and repairing, hydraulic systems, power-operated, air, and vacuum brakes)	500
c. Chassis (frames, steering units, front suspension systems, shock absorbers, and springs)	750
d. Clutches and transmissions (standard and automatic transmissions, overdrives and shift controls, and power take-off)	1,250
e. Rear axle assembly (differential, universal joints, drivelines, rear axle)	750
f. Power plants (valves, timing gears and chains, piston and ring assembly, bearing and crankshaft, cylinder reconditioning)	1,500
g. Electric system (wire and light system, alternator, generator and regulator, starting motors, windshield wipers, instruments and gauges, ignition and battery, transmission controls)	1,000
h. Motor analyzing (carburetors, fuel systems, distributors, troubleshooting, fuel injectors, tune-up)	1,000

   i. Exhaust emission controls (exhaust analyzers,
     catalytic converters, controls, pumps)   300
   j. Miscellaneous (exhaust systems, welding, auxiliary devices,
     shop operations, service, selling, and supervision review)   450
Total   **8,000 hours**

For every three journeymen employed, there should be one apprentice. For example, if the shop employs from one to three journeymen, it should have one apprentice. If the shop employs four to six journeymen, it should employ two apprentices, and so on. Pay is based on a percentage of the journeyman's scale and rises from 55 percent to 90 percent of scale through the four years of apprenticeship.

Auto Body Technician

A four-year apprenticeship program for automobile body technicians might be arranged as follows:

Recommended Work-Experience Schedule   *Approximate Hours*

   a. Shop Routine: using and maintaining typical shop tools
     and equipment, shop safety practices, and exposure
     to basic mechanical concepts and procedures.   500
   b. Basic Metal: disassembling, assembling, and aligning;
     roughing small dents with a hammer and dolly; dinging
     small dents with a pick and file; metal shrinking;
     welding and brazing; soldering; plastic filling;
     and repairing large dents using all of the above procedures.   1,500
   c. Advanced Metal Work: repairing door panels, rocker panels,
     quarter panels, trunk lids, and hoods; installing doors,
     trunk lids, and hoods; and transferring all necessary parts.   1,500
   d. Refinishing: compounding, polishing, and waxing
     automotive finishes; feather-edging metal finished areas;
     properly using masking tape; applying primer-surfacer
     and glazing putty and sanding these materials; refinishing
     body panels with enamel-type paint; two-phase painting
     (color and clear); refinishing nonsteel body panels including
     polyurethane, aluminum, and fiberglass.   1,000

e. Basic Auto Body Rebuilding: repairing top cowl panels,
   cowl posts, and firewalls; repairing body and trunk floors
   and seats; repairing turret tops, including rear glass and
   windshield openings; installing quarter panels, door panels,
   and rocker panels.   1,500
f. Major Auto Body Rebuilding: repairing frame horns;
   repairing frames from under rear seat to rear cross member
   on unibody structures and conventional frames; repairing
   frame from cowl forward to frame horns; repairing bumpers
   and mounting structures; transferring and being responsible
   for major component and subassemblies, such as suspensions,
   engines, and related parts; drivetrain, rear axle, and braking;
   air-conditioning and cooling systems.   2,000

Recommended Wage Schedule

The recommended wage schedule for the apprentice auto body technician is the same as for the automotive technician. The program, which takes four years (eight thousand hours), is divided by one-thousand-hour increments with the apprentice's wages being the same percentage of the journeyman's as shown for the auto mechanic. The average wage percentage over the course of the program is 72.5 percent.

Recommended Apprentice Ratio

Just as for the automobile mechanic, the recommended ratio of apprentices to journeymen is one to three. For example, if the shop employs from one to three journeymen, it should have one apprentice. If the shop employs seven to nine journeymen, it should employ three apprentices.

Automobile Painter or Refinisher

The final category covers the automobile painter. The apprenticeship program takes only three years or six thousand hours to complete. Following is the breakdown of the time and schedule of experiences for the auto painter.

Automobile Painter

Recommended Work-Experience Schedule	*Approximate Hours*
a. Miscellaneous	400
b. Cleaning equipment and metal surfaces to be painted	600
c. Rough sanding of repair or rust spots	500
d. Masking around panels to be painted	500
e. Removing paint	500
f. Sanding intermediate coats	500
g. Rubbing and polishing finished coat	500
h. Adjusting spray gun and spraying intermediate coats	800
i. Adjusting spray gun and spraying finished coats	400
j. Brush touching	300
k. Spot or patch repairing and mixing paints	1,000
Total	**6,000 hours**

APPRENTICESHIP TODAY

Although the number of formal apprenticeships may be down, the informal apprenticeships that happen in a workplace also can be helpful. If you're in a unionized field, your chances of finding a formal program are better. The International Association of Machinists and Aerospace Workers, the United Auto Workers, and other unions may have more information on the subject.

Here is an apprenticeship program (2001) that's worked in St. Louis, Missouri. It was developed by car dealers, truck dealers, and the International Association of Machinists, along with the U.S. Department of labor. The program has an enrollment of 50 to 70 a year, but it can place as many as 150 to 200 apprentices!

Automobile Mechanic

Work Process Summary	*Approximate Hours*
1. Chassis and springs	800
2. Front axle and steering	1,000
3. Rear wheel and axle assembly	1,000
4. Transmission and clutch	1,000
5. Motor	2,000

6. Brakes	600
7. Tune-up (includes: fuel systems, ignition, electrical, cooling, fuel pump, and air-conditioning)	1,600
8. Review and miscellaneous (not to exceed 25 percent of the number of hours worked during any quarter)	____
Total	**8,000**

Body Repair Mechanic

Work Process Summary	*Approximate Hours*
1. Perform MIG (GMAW) heating and welding techniques	500
2. Working with trim and hardware	500
3. Replace and align panels	2,000
a. quarter panels	
b. partial and/or full panels	
4. Straighten metal	1,500
5. Use body fillers	500
6. Replace door skin and intrusion beams	500
7. Repair and replace movable glass and hardware	500
8. Complete structural repair using various types of pulling and measuring tools	1,000
9. Replace stationary glass	500
10. Restore corrosion protection	500
11. Review and miscellaneous (not to exceed 25 percent of the number of hours worked during any quarter)	____
Total	**8,000**

Truck Mechanic

Work Process Summary	*Approximate Hours*
1. Chassis lubrication	100
2. Brakes—hydraulic, air, mechanical, and power; relining, adjusting, and general repair; burnishing and painting brake shoes; installing air brakes and vacuum brakes; installing air lines tanks and cylinders	1,000

3. Front end suspension and steering 1,900
   a. Theory and adjustment of camber, caster, toe in
      and out; backward or forward tilt of king pins;
      king pin inclination.
   b. Wheel alignment: theory, diagnosing trouble,
      and alignment; straighten and replace axles
   c. Wheel balancing: remove and replace wheels;
      read meter and install weights to balance wheels
      and tires, statically and dynamically
4. Frame work 1,400
   a. Conversion work
      1. lengthening or shortening frames and
         drive shafts
      2. change axle assembly
      3. install extra gas tanks
      4. install overload springs
      5. install fifth wheel
      6. chassis assembly
      7. repair and straighten frames
      8. rear wheel and axle assembly
5. Welding: electric, acetylene, spot, cutting, and brazing 500
6. Electric system: study wire diagram; install and repair
   lighting equipment, signals, etc. 400
7. Transmission and clutch 1,000
8. Diesel and gas engines (repair): engine tune-up
   including fuel systems, ignition, electrical, cooling,
   fuel pumps, and air-conditioning 1,000
9. Knowledge and use of special tools and equipment:
   special frame tools, air tools, air-ride equipment
   tools, special front-end tools, etc. 500
10. Miscellaneous and review 200

Total   **8,000**

Automotive Machinist

Work Process Summary	*Approximate Hours*
1. Disassemble engine and clean parts	200

2 Engine rebuilding
  a. Cylinder blocks   600
    1. boring cylinders
    2. honing cylinders
    3. piston pin fittings
    4. piston fittings
    5. piston ring fittings
    6. install cylinder sleeves
  b. Bearings   1,200
    1. main bearings
      a. boring to size
      b. fitting
      c. installation
    2. camshaft bearings
      a. boring to size
      b. fitting
      c. installation
    3. connecting rod bearings
      a. boring to size
      b. fitting
      c. installation
  c. Valves   1,200
    1. reseating
    2. new seat installation
    3. adjusting tappets
  d. Oil pumps   200
    1. disassemble
    2. repair and replace worn parts
    3. assemble
  e. Transmissions   1,200
    1. disassemble
    2. check gears and shafts
    3. replace worn parts
    4. assemble
  f. Universal joint—rebuilding   200
    1. Detroit joints
    2. mechanical joints

3. Cleveland joints
4. spicer joints
g. Cold welding   200
1. cylinder heads
2. cylinder blocks
h. Brake rebuilding   1,200
1. hydraulic and mechanical
   a. disassemble
   b. replace worn cylinder parts
   c. reline brake shoes
   d. brake shoe reconditioning
i. Crankshaft grinding   800
1. stationary
2. portable
j. General shop work   1,000
1. lathe
2. borer
3. drill press
4. grinder

Total   **8,000**

CHAPTER 14

TECHNICIAN CERTIFICATION

If you are interested in autos and how they work, and you must be if you are reading this book, you have probably been asked more than once, "Where can I find a good mechanic?"

Whom can a person trust? Who has the proper skills and knowledge? It is very difficult to tell. There has been much talk lately regarding the licensing of automobile repair people, but is that the way things should be? Is that how they will be?

Perhaps licensing will be a fact of life for the technician of the future all across the nation. Canada licenses its motor vehicle mechanics in a program supervised by provincial governments. The state of Michigan has already adopted an automotive technician licensing program. It may be the only solution to a bad situation, or at least the most palatable of alternatives.

NATIONAL INSTITUTE FOR AUTOMOTIVE
SERVICE EXCELLENCE (ASE)

At present the best solution is voluntary certification of those in the automotive trade. There is only one certification program in the nation that is recognized by everyone in the industry. It is called the National Institute for Automotive Service Excellence (ASE).

Before 1972 there was no such organization as the National Institute for Automotive Service Excellence. Initially it was funded by the "Big Four" automakers in the United States: General Motors, Ford, Chrysler, and American

Motors. The new-car dealers' association also helped get the program started. Since that time, independent garage owners, service station operators, after-market wholesalers, manufacturers, and distributors have joined the band-wagon. Pick up any trade publication in this industry, and you will probably find an endorsement at the bottom of most advertisements for ASE.

The institute no longer needs the financial assistance once provided by the automakers. It is entirely self-supporting, with all of its funds coming from the modest test fees charged.

The institute's goal is to organize and promote the highest standards of automotive service in the public interest. It conducts continuing research to determine the best methods for training automotive technicians, encourages the development of effective training programs, and evaluates the competence of technicians through a testing and certification program.

In May and November of every year the tests for mechanic certification are administered simultaneously to applicants all over the country in more than 650 locations. The tests are usually administered at a high school, community college, or technical institute in the area. This arrangement, coupled with the fact that the tests are changed each time they are administered, ensures tight security. They are probably the most closely controlled tests conducted in the country. In some cases a special test center may be established. If there is no test center within fifty miles, a group of at least twenty persons may get together and request a special test center. Once the special center is estab-lished, others in the area may register to take the tests there.

The tests are written by automotive engineers, working technicians, voca-tional instructors, and automotive trade press editors who are brought together by the institute. The "raw" questions are then rewritten and put into profes-sionally acceptable format by the American College Testing Program (ACT) of Iowa City, Iowa.

After the questions are assembled, they are tried out on panels of working technicians, engineers, and other experts who critique the questions and elim-inate those that are ambiguous, tricky, or not "real world." Then, and only then, are the questions approved and made a part of the forthcoming tests.

Although anyone who pays the test fees may take the tests, only those individuals with two or more years of experience as a working technician will receive ASE certification. There is one exception: Up to one year's credit can be given for specific vocational schooling, where sufficient shop-time work can be documented.

No special training is necessary, however, since the tests are designed for working technicians. The tests reflect the technicians' expertise in the areas that they work on every day.

For example, if a technician principally does brake and front-end work, in two or three years he or she should have little trouble with those two tests. However, if the person has not done much engine work for two or three years and wishes to take the engine test, it would be a good idea to take a refresher course in engines.

This can help upgrade the expertise of practicing technicians to the benefit not only of themselves but also of the motorists who trust their vehicles to them.

THE TESTS

There are eight tests for the general automotive technician: engine repair, automatic transmission/transaxle, manual drive train and axles, suspension and steering, brakes, electrical systems, heating and air-conditioning, and engine performance (which was previously called engine tune-up).

In addition, there are eight tests for heavy-duty truck mechanics, and five tests for auto body repairers and painters.

All tests are multiple choice and are problem oriented. For example, a test question might be, "A vehicle with a computer-controlled (feedback) engine has poor gas mileage. Engine tests show a rich mixture. Technician A says that a bad oxygen (O_2) sensor could be the cause. Technician B says that a bad intake air temperature sensor could be the cause. Who is right?"

A. A only
B. B only
C. Both A and B
D. Neither A nor B

For anyone who is very familiar with the particular area being tested, the tests may seem rather easy. Other tests may seem extremely difficult. This simply points out the technician's weakness in one area and confirms expertise in another. The tests can be taken any number of times as long as the applicant pays the test fee. It is a good barometer of how well he or she knows his or her stuff. It is also a great way to force oneself to learn what is needed to pass a particular test.

The duty task lists given here are only in outline form. Some categories are expanded to show more detail. For the full list of requirements, together with sample questions and answers, contact ASE.

Automobile Technician

Engine Repair (Test A1)

    A. General engine diagnosis

    B. Cylinder head and valve train diagnosis and repair

    C. Engine block diagnosis and repair

    D. Lubrication and cooling system diagnosis and repair

    E. Fuel, electrical, ignition, and exhaust systems inspection and service

Engine Performance (Test A8)

    A. General engine diagnosis

    B. Ignition system diagnosis and repair

    C. Fuel, air induction, and exhaust systems diagnosis and repair

    D. Emissions control systems diagnosis and repair

    E. Computerized engine controls diagnosis and repair

        1. Diagnose the causes of emissions problems resulting from failure of computerized engine controls.

        2. Perform analytic/diagnostic procedures on vehicles with on-board diagnostic computer systems; determine needed action.

        3. Inspect, test, adjust, and replace sensor, control, and actuator components and circuits of computerized engine control systems.

        4. Use and interpret digital multimeter (DMM) readings.

        5. Read and interpret technical literature (service publications and information).

        6. Test, remove, inspect, clean, service, and repair or replace power distribution circuits and connections.

7. Practice recommended precautions when handling static sensitive devices.

8. Diagnose drivability and emissions problems resulting from failures of inter-dependent systems (security alarms, torque controls, suspension controls, traction controls, torque management, A/C, and similar systems).

F. Engine electrical systems diagnosis and repair.

Medium/Heavy Truck Technician

Diesel Engine (Test T2)

A. General engine diagnosis

B. Cylinder head and valve train diagnosis and repair

C. Engine block diagnosis and repair

D. Lubrication and cooling system diagnosis and repair

E. Air induction and exhaust systems diagnosis and repair

F. Fuel system diagnosis and repair

G. Starting system diagnosis and repair

H. Engine brakes

Collision Repair and Refinishing

Painting and Refinishing (Test B2)

A. Surface preparation

B. Spray gun operation and related equipment

C. Paint mixing, matching, and applying

D. Solving paint application problems

E. Finish defects, causes, and cures

F. Safety precautions and miscellaneous

Structural Analysis and Damage Repair (Test B4)

A. Frame inspection and repair

B. Unibody inspection, measurement, and repair

C. Stationary glass

D. Metal welding and cutting

BENEFITS

The institute strongly believes that certification helps everyone. The technicians gain prestige and recognition, and their value to their employers is definitely increased. The test results let technicians know areas of strength as well as weaknesses, so they can decide where additional training is needed.

Employers benefit because they can market certified technicians to customers. The institute provides signs advertising that an employer hires technicians who are certified by the ASE. The employer also uses this to advantage in media advertising. But the most important benefit is to the consumer, the motoring public. The motorists benefit because they now can look for and choose a mechanic who has proven skills, as opposed to one who just claims to be a mechanic. The motorist can tell at a glance who is a bona fide technician.

RECOGNITION

Recognition of a certified technician comes in two ways. The first is the recognition from fellow technicians in the trade. The second is from the public. It is easy to spot a certified technician. He or she wears a blue-and-white shoulder patch on his or her work uniform. Persons who have passed all eight tests are awarded certified master automobile technician status. A gold bar on their patch states so.

The motorist need not walk (or drive) right up to the technician but only needs to look for a sign outside the shop that proclaims: "We employ technicians certified by ASE—let us show you their credentials."

TO BECOME CERTIFIED

Today there are more than 425,000 technicians who have been certified by the National Institute for Automotive Service Excellence. ASE has become the major voluntary automotive technician certification program throughout the nation and has been increasingly accepted by legislators and the public alike. Recertification (every five years) ensures the continued integrity and validity of ASE credentials. If you are interested in becoming a certified technician, you can get more information by writing:

National Institute for Automotive Service Excellence
13505 Dulles Technology Drive, Suite 2
Herndon, VA 20171-3421

TEST AIDS

There are a number of very good aids for persons interested in taking the ASE tests. Check the ASE website for links to preparation and training materials.

One package is available from Chek-Chart, which offers a complete automobile technician's refresher course. The complete set is designed as a self-instruction course in theory and practical application for all of the automotive systems. Write:

Chek-Chart Products
Attn: Order Dept.
5600 Crooks Road, Suite 200
Troy, MI 48098

Another is from Nichols Publishing, which publishes *Chilton's Automotive Repair*. Write to:

Nichols Publishing
1025 Andrew Drive, Suite 100
West Chester, PA 19380-4291
www.chiltonsonline.com

CHAPTER 15

WHAT DOES IT PAY?

In general, automotive service technicians enjoy their work and earn a good wage. Most beginners, however, start working at the minimum wage. A classic example is the high school student who works after school at the local service station. He or she may do more chores around the station than automotive service, but those are the dues one has to pay. Few people begin climbing the ladder of success in the middle. Although the chores are important, the greater advantage is the opportunity to observe and learn shop practices and become familiar with the environment of the auto repair shop. This experience, coupled with the minimum wage, is how you pay your dues.

The automotive apprentice also may start at close to the minimum wage, but the advantage is that he or she will be learning actual repair and service techniques. Once the apprentice has passed the probationary period, raises will come. After the first six months of training, the apprentice makes 55 percent of the journeyman's wage; at the end of the four-year apprenticeship program, he or she is making almost 75 percent of what the journeyman earns.

The sky is the limit for the top-notch technician. Once he or she has achieved journeyman status, most of the work performed is paid on a flat-rate basis—that is, each job function is assigned a certain amount of time in which it should be done. *Motor Service* magazine recently found in an informal survey that about 60 percent of shops used the flat-rate system, while 40 percent paid on a salary-and-bonus basis. The flat-rate evolved as an incentive to productivity. If the technician is able to complete the job in less time than allocated, he or she is still paid for the full amount. For example, the flat-rate schedule for replacing the water pump on a certain engine may provide for 2.3

hours of labor time. If the technician does the job in 2.0 hours, he or she is still paid 2.3 hours' worth of wages for that job. For the exceptional technician it is not uncommon to complete every job in less time than the book stipulates. If the technician can do ten hours' worth of work in eight hours, he or she is paid for ten hours' worth of work.

The flat-rate schedule is both a benefit and a problem. If the technician runs into a problem that delays the job, he or she still only gets paid for the given time. Take four hours to do a two-hour job, and all you will get paid for is two hours' worth of work. Flat-rate schedules, however, are usually the average time a job should take, and the technician should seldom lose out.

The flat-rate schedule also benefits the customer. Based on the time allowances, the service manager or service adviser can estimate the customer's bill quite accurately before the work is performed.

Almost all technicians meet or beat the flat-rate times. A technician who consistently comes in over the time will not last too long in that shop. He or she will either get disgusted and leave, or the supervisor will replace him or her with someone who is more efficient. In 1999, the top 10 percent of U.S. auto technicians earned an average hourly wage of $22.17. Average wages for all auto technicians were almost $14.00 an hour. With computer diagnostic skills, technicians can earn between $30,000 and $75,000 annually. The AYES program surveyed its national network of dealers and found the high end of salaries had topped $105,000 a year.

Salaries in the Major Automotive Service Businesses
(Hourly and Annual, Low-End to High-End Salaries and Mean)

Occupation	10th%	25th%	50th%	75th%	90th%	Mean Wages
Auto service	$7.74	$10.30	$13.62	$17.79	$22.17	$14.49
technicians	$16,090	$21,420	$28,330	$37,010	$46,110	$30,130
Auto body	$8.32	$11.30	$15.06	$20.03	$25.81	$16.21
repairers	$17,310	$23,500	$31,310	$41,670	$53,690	$33,720
Auto glass	$7.20	$9.79	$13.26	$16.01	$19.91	$13.34
installers/repairers	$14,970	$20,350	$27,570	$33,300	$41,410	$27,740

Occupation	10th%	25th%	50th%	75th%	90th%	Mean Wages
Bus and truck mechanics and diesel engine specialists	$9.72 $20,220	$11.76 $24,470	$14.77 $30,720	$18.29 $38,030	$21.50 $44,730	$15.29 $31,800
Farm equipment mechanics	$7.34 $15,260	$9.22 $19,190	$11.42 $23,750	$14.00 $29,110	$16.85 $35,060	$11.91 $24,770
Mobile heavy equipment mechanics	$10.51 $21,860	$12.62 $26,250	$15.75 $32,770	$19.16 $39,850	$22.53 $46,860	$16.24 $33,790
Motorcycle mechanics	$7.16 $14,890	$9.32 $19,390	$11.61 $24,140	$14.81 $30,790	$18.21 $37,870	$12.26 $25,510
Painters of transport equipment	$8.61 $17,900	$10.96 $22,790	$14.13 $29,380	$19.21 $39,950	$23.87 $49,650	$15.36 $31,940
Recreational vehicle service technicians	$8.08 $16,800	$9.65 $20,070	$11.86 $24,670	$14.51 $30,170	$17.25 $35,870	$12.49 $25,980
Service station attendants	$5.72 $11,900	$6.12 $12,730	$7.11 $14,780	$8.38 $17,430	$10.08 $20,980	$7.58 $15,770

Source: Bureau of Labor Statistics, 1999 National Occupational Employment and Wage Estimates. Percentile wage estimates show what percentage of workers in an occupation earns less than a given wage and what percentage earns more. www.bls.gov/oes/1999/oes493023.htm

SERVICE STATION ATTENDANT

As mentioned earlier, the position of service station attendant is an entry-level one. The range of earnings can cover quite a spread, and wages vary from place to place in the country. According to the Career Information Center, the service station attendant earns minimum wage salaries, or less, to start. It is common for attendants to be paid a commission on top of their hourly wage as an incentive and reward for sales ability. Some service station owners or managers devise unique incentive programs for their employees that may help to supplement their wages.

AUTOMOTIVE SERVICE ADVISER

Automobile service advisers are paid an hourly wage that is usually one-third higher than the average for all nonsupervisory workers employed in private industry. Many service advisers are paid an extra amount in the form of commissions. They usually receive a percentage of the cost of all repairs and accessories that the customer pays for. Some service advisers are paid on a straight commission basis. This is quite common for those who are employed by mass merchandisers and department stores that offer automotive service. In order to make good money in this kind of business, the person employed as a service adviser must have excellent sales ability.

AUTOMOTIVE PARTS SPECIALIST

The typical automotive parts specialist works forty to forty-eight hours a week. Although some workers work a basic nine-to-five job, many more will end up with shifts where they will work some evenings and weekends to accommodate their customers.

Usually parts specialists are paid hourly wages starting at minimum wage for the many part-timers in this field, although some are salaried and others earn commissions. The parts specialist at automobile dealerships usually gets a commission based on the volume of parts and service work performed by the technicians. Outside salespeople are frequently paid a commission, and sometimes they get bonuses if they land a new account. The best career opportunities are in management of a parts store, either wholesale or retail.

AUTOMOBILE BODY REPAIRER

As with most craft professions, the earnings of the automobile body repair person are quite good, about one and three-fourths times the average for persons employed in private industry who do not have management positions. The highly skilled body repairer may expect to earn as much as 30 to

60 percent more than what an unskilled helper or trainee makes. Yearly earnings can be in the range of $25,000 to $50,000, according to estimates from the Automotive Service Association (ASA).

If the body repair specialist works for an automobile dealer, he or she is usually paid a commission. In this way the earnings depend on the amount of work there is and how fast the repair person can get it done. Commissioned workers are usually given a promised salary or wage, but it is usually much lower than he or she can expect to make in an average week.

Helpers, trainees, and apprentices are usually paid by the hour until they become proficient enough to work on a commission basis. Those who work for private fleets are usually paid an hourly wage rather than a commission, since there is no retail trade through the shop. The average workweek is forty to forty-eight hours, with very few weekend or evening hours in the schedule.

AUTOMOBILE PAINTER

Based on a survey of painters working in the thirty-six large metropolitan U.S. cities, the average hourly earnings were $13.57 per hour. This compares quite favorably to other nonsupervisory workers in private industry. Of course, beginners and inexperienced workers and apprentices earn considerably less. The more experienced the person is, the better his or her wages are. ASA estimated the annual salary range as $25,000 to $50,000.

Many of the painters working for automobile dealerships are paid a commission similar to that paid to body repair persons. Earnings on the commission basis depend to a great extent on the amount of work done and how fast the person performs the work. This system is often a disadvantage to a slow or less-skilled and inexperienced person. For the experienced worker, however, it provides an opportunity for a very handsome income. Often a weekly salary is guaranteed, but it is usually minimal.

Trainees and helpers are usually paid on an hourly basis until they become proficient and sufficiently skilled to switch to the commission plan. Automobile painters are often employed by larger fleets, such as taxi companies, delivery firms, and trucking companies. Trucking companies, bus lines, and taxi companies that maintain their own staff of mechanics and painters usually pay their employees an hourly wage or salary. Most automotive painters work forty to forty-eight hours a week and seldom work evenings or weekends.

CAREER NETWORK RESOURCES FOR AUTOMOTIVE SERVICES

EDUCATIONAL RESOURCES

Accrediting Commission of Career Schools and Colleges of Technology
2101 Wilson Boulevard, Suite 302
Arlington, VA 22201

A private, nonprofit group that publishes an annual directory of schools and colleges in the United States. Schools that belong must meet its standards.

Association of Canadian Community Colleges
Michael Street North, Suite 200-1223
Ottawa, Ontario K1J 7T2
www.accc.ca/english

Many Canadian colleges offer an auto repair degree or certificate.

Automotive Youth Education Systems (AYES), Inc.
2701 Troy Center Drive, Suite 450
Troy, MI 48084
www.ayes.org

This is the biggest national school-to-work program, organized and sponsored by major auto and truck manufacturers, dealers, toolmakers, and auto parts suppliers. Hundreds of high schools are now participating.

FinAid Page, LLC
P.O. Box 81620
Pittsburgh, PA 15217
www.FAFSA.org

Offers financial aid information on government-sponsored loans; standard forms for college financial aid applications, the Free Application for Federal Student Aid (FAFSA).

National Automotive Technicians Education Foundation (NATEF)
13505 Dulles Technology Drive
Herndon, VA 20171-3421
www.natef.org

Find the complete list of ASE-certified schools and colleges at this website. You can search by specialty or geography for auto, auto body, truck, bus, and other training programs at high schools and colleges.

National Institute for Automotive Service Excellence
13505 Dulles Technology Drive, Suite 2
Herndon, VA 20171-3421
www.asecert.org

Provides information on auto, auto body, truck, and bus technician careers. This organization tests and certifies auto and truck technicians and other automotive service occupations. Maintains a list of schools that train technicians to their program standards.

SkillsUSA-VICA
P.O. Box 3000
1401 James Monroe Highway
Leesburg, VA 22075
www.skillsusa.org

Provides information on technical careers and education and a directory of public training programs for diesel mechanics and service technicians.

CAR MANUFACTURERS' EDUCATION PROGRAMS

Chrysler CAP
DaimlerChrysler Motors Corp.
Dealer Technical Operations
2367 Walton Boulevard
CIMS 428-00-00
Auburn Hills, MI 48326-1955
www.CAP.daimlerchryslercorp.com

Ford Asset
www.fordasset.com

GM ASEP/BSEP
1650 Research Drive, Suite 200
Troy, MI 48083
www.gmstc.com
www.gmstc.com/asep-bsep

The International Association of General Motors Automotive Service
Educational Programs (ASEP) has sixty-five technical colleges and universi-
ties in the United States and sixteen in Canada.

Honda Professional Automotive Career Training (PACT)
Honda Industrial Education Liaison
American Honda Motor Company
1919 Torrance Boulevard
Mail Stop 500-2C-11B
Torrance, CA 90501

Nissan Professional Cooperative Apprenticeship Program
(PROCAP)
Nissan PROCAP
P.O. Box 191
Gardena, CA 90248

Toyota T-Ten
Technical Education Network (T-TEN)
19001 South Western Avenue
Torrance, CA 90509
www.t-ten.com

TEACHER/TRAINER ORGANIZATIONS

Council of Advanced Automotive Trainers
632 Gamble Drive
Lisle, IL 60532
www.caat.org

Industry Planning Council
c/o American Automobile Manufacturers Association
3011 West Grand Boulevard, Suite 407
Detroit, MI 48202-3011

North American Council of Auto Teachers
11956 Bernardo Plaza Drive, Department 436
San Diego, CA 92128-9713

AUTO BODY REPAIR

I-Car Education Foundation
(Interindustry Conference on Auto Collision Repair)
3701 Algonquin Road, Suite 400
Rolling Meadows, IL 60008
www.i-car.com

Provides information on careers in collision repair as well as training courses and programs.

National Association of Automotive Trim and Restyling Shops
6255 Barfield Road, #200
Atlanta, GA 30328-4300

PROFESSIONAL ENGINEERING GROUPS AND SOCIETIES

Institute of Transportation Engineers
525 School Street SW, Suite 410
Washington, D.C. 20024-2797

Society of Automotive Engineers
400 Commonwealth Drive
Warrendale, PA 15096-0001
www.sae.org

TOOL MANUFACTURERS

Mac Tools
Customer Service Department
4635 Hilton Corporate Drive
Columbus, OH 43232
www.mactools.com

Matco Tools
4403 Allen Road
Stow, OH 44244

Sears, Roebuck and Company
333 Beverly Road
Hoffman Estates, IL 60179
www.sears.com

Snap-on Inc.
P.O. Box 1410
Kenosha, WI 53141
www.snapon.com

(Note: Many other fine brands of tools are available. Check Tool and Equipment Institute, www.etools.org, for more information.)

DIESEL ENGINE/TRUCK MANUFACTURERS

Cummins Engine Company, Inc.
Box 3005
Columbus, IN 47202-3005
www.cummins.com

Detroit Diesel
Personnel Director MS B39
13400 West Outer Drive
Detroit, MI 48239

Kenworth Truck Company
Service Coordinator
700 East Gate Drive, Suite 325
Mt. Laurel, NJ 08054

GOVERNMENT

Bureau of Labor Statistics
www.bls.gov

Gives information on careers and labor statistics from the government's best number-crunchers. The *Occupational Outlook Handbook* is now on-line.

Volpe Transportation Strategic Planning and Analysis Office
www.volpe.dot.gov

Provides research on the future of transportation in the United States and worldwide.

ASSOCIATIONS

U.S. ORGANIZATIONS

American Trucking Association
2200 Mill Road
Alexandria, VA 22314-4677

Auto Body Parts Association
P.O. Box 820689
Houston, TX 77282-0689

AutoBody Craftsman Association
1124 Industry Drive
Tukwila, WA 98188

Automotive Aftermarket Industry Association
4600 East West Highway, Suite 300
Bethesda, MD 20814-3415
www.aftermarket.org

Automotive Maintenance and Repair Association
1444 I Street, Suite 700
Washington, D.C. 20005

Automotive Service Association
1901 Airport Freeway
Bedford, TX 76021-5732
www.asashop.org

This is a national group dedicated to auto service repair shops.

CCAR
10901 Lowell Avenue, Suite 201
Overland Park, KS 66210
www.ccar-greenlink.org

Provides information on automotive career education. It is also an on-line career center with many links to information about environmental compliance (controlling pollution from engines), emissions control specialty companies, and organizations.

Council of Fleet Specialists
315 Delaware Street
Kansas City, MO 64105
www.cfshq.com

The council is composed of heavy-duty truck parts and service distributors.

Dismantlers and Recyclers of America
Automotive Recyclers Association
3975 Fair Ridge Drive, Suite 20
Terrace Level-North
Fairfax, VA 22033-2924

Equipment and Tool Institute
P.O. Box 13966
10 Laboratory Drive
Research Triangle Park, NC 27709-3966
www.etools.org

Motor and Equipment Manufacturers Association
10 Laboratory Drive
P.O. Box 13966
Research Triangle Park, NC 27709-3966
www.mema.org

National Association of Truck Stop Owners (NATSO)
1199 North Fairfax Street, Suite 801
Alexandria, VA 22314

National Auto Dealers Association (NADA)
8400 Westpark Drive
McLean, VA 22102
www.nada.org

National Automotive Parts Association
2999 Circle 75 Parkway
Atlanta, GA 30339-3050

National Truck Equipment Association
37400 Hills Tech Drive
Farmington Hills, MI 48331-3414
www.ntea.com

Owner-Operators Independent Drivers Association (Trucks)
P.O. Box L
Grain Valley, MO 64029
www.ooida.com

Truck Manufacturers Association
1225 New York Avenue NW, Suite 300
Washington, D.C. 20005

UNIONS

International Association of Machinists and Aerospace Workers
9000 Machinists Place
Upper Marlboro, MD 20772-2687
www.iamaw.org

The association provides information on apprenticeship programs and union-related jobs for machinists and other automotive careers.

United Auto Workers (UAW)
8000 East Jefferson
Detroit, MI 48214
www.uaw.org

UAW-Big Three National Training Centers:

The UAW-DaimlerChrysler National Training Center
2211 East Jefferson Avenue
Detroit, MI 48207

The UAW-Ford National Programs Center
151 West Jefferson
P.O. Box 33009
Detroit, MI 48232

The UAW-GM Human Resources Center
2630 Featherstone Road
Auburn Hills, MI 48326

CANADA

Auto Parts Manufacturers Association (APMA)
195 The West Mall, Suite 516
Toronto, ON M9C 5K1
www.capma.com

Apprentice registration is either compulsory or voluntary for automotive mechanics, depending on provincial law.

Automotive Industries Association of Canada
1272 Wellington
Ottawa, ON K1Y 3A7
www.aiacanada.com

Includes wholesalers and manufacturers of auto parts and accessories. Has a scholarship fund.

SPECIALTY ORGANIZATIONS

AED Foundation
Associated Equipment Dealers
615 West Twenty-Second Street
Oak Brook, IL 60523
www.aednet.org

The Equipment Maintenance Council
2020 Lake Shore Court
Sanger, TX 76266

Provides information about careers in mobile heavy equipment maintenance.

North American Equipment Dealers Association
10877 Watson Road
St. Louis, MO 63127

Provides farm equipment work opportunities. You also should contact local farm equipment dealers and state employment service offices.

Specialized Carriers and Rigging Association
2750 Prosperity Avenue, Suite 620
Fairfax, VA 22031-4312
www.scranet.org

Is concerned with mobile heavy equipment maintenance.

APPENDIX C

FOR MORE INFORMATION

PUBLICATIONS

Automotive News
www.automotivenews.com

A weekly newspaper of the auto industry published by Crain Communications.

Motor Service
www.autotruck.net

A trade magazine devoted to the auto service industry.

WEBSITES

Note: Website addresses do change occasionally. If that happens, try using a search engine to find the organization name you're looking for.

Association for Career & Technician Education
www.acteonline.org

Provides information about education for technical careers.

www.autotechnicians.com

Provides information for technicians and auto shop managers.

www.autotruck.net

Provides publications and links related to automotive service.

www.motorist.org

A consumer site with auto repair information from the consumer's viewpoint. (Can be an eye-opener for auto technicians!) Offers recommended standards of service for repair shops. Also has good links to auto-related information.

EDUCATIONAL INSTITUTIONS

This list is a sample of schools and colleges offering automotive technology certificates and degrees. It is compiled from the U.S. Department of Education's IPEDS COOL list, which can be found at www.cd.gov/global-locator. You can search there by state, zip code, and other search terms. Many, but not all, of the schools are certified by the ASE. If you wish to attend an ASE-certified school, check the official list of ASE-certified schools at www.natef.org. Their list includes both high schools and college-level programs, with indications of which manufacturers' programs are offered. You can search by specialty—auto, medium/heavy truck, body repair, etc. The ASE list is too extensive to be reprinted here.

UNITED STATES

Alabama
Shelton State Community College
9500 Old Greensboro Road
Tuscaloosa, AL 35405
www.shelton.cc.al.us

Alaska
Alaska Vocational Technical Center
809 Second Avenue
Seward, AK 99664
www.educ.state.ak.us/avtec

University of Alaska, Anchorage
3211 Providence Drive
Anchorage, AK 99508

Arizona
Arizona Automotive Institute
6829 North Forty-Sixth Avenue
Glendale, AZ 85301-3579
www.azautoinst.com

Universal Technical Institute, Inc.
3121 West Weldon Avenue
Phoenix, AZ 85017
http://uticorp.com

Arkansas
Great Rivers Vocational Technical School
1609 East Ash
McGehee, AR 71654
http://grti.tec.ar.us

Northwest Technical Institute
709 South Old Missouri Road
Springdale, AR 72764
www.nti.tec.ar.us

California
American River College
4700 College Oak Drive
Sacramento, CA 95841-4286
www.arc.losrios.cc.ca.us/

Los Angeles Trade Technical College
400 West Washington Boulevard
Los Angeles, CA 90015-4181

Colorado
Arapahoe Community College
5900 South Santa Fe Drive
P.O. Box 9002
Littleton, CO 80160-9002
www.arapahoe.edu

Denver Automotive and Diesel College
460 South Lipan Street
Denver, CO 80223-9366
www.DenverAutoDiesel.com

Connecticut
Baran Institute of Technology
611 Day Hill Road
Windsor, CT 06095
www.baraninstitute.com

New England Technical Institute of Connecticut, Inc.
200 John Downey Drive
New Britain, CT 06051
http://GONewEnglandTech.com

Delaware
Delaware Technical and Community College, Owens
P.O. Box 610
Georgetown, DE 19947

Delaware Technical & Community College, Stanton-Wilmington
400 Stanton-Christiana Road
Newark, DE 19702

Florida
Lindsey Hopkins Technical Education Center
750 NW Twentieth Street
Miami, FL 33127
www.dade.k12.fl.us/lindsey

Lorenzo Walker Institute of Technology
3702 Estey Avenue
Naples, FL 34104

Georgia
Atlanta Technical College
1560 Metropolitan Parkway SW
Atlanta, GA 30310-4446
www.atlantatech.org/

Columbus Technical College
928 Manchester Expressway
Columbus, GA 31904-6572
www.columbustech.org

Hawaii
Honolulu Community College
874 Dillingham Boulevard
Honolulu, HI 96817
www.hcc.hawaii.edu

Leeward Community College
96-045 ALA IKE
Pearl City, HI 96782
www.lcc.hawaii.edu

Idaho
Boise State University
1910 University Drive
Boise, ID 83725-1135
www.boisestate.edu

Idaho State University
741 South Seventh Avenue
Pocatello, ID 83209
www.isu.edu/home.shtml

Illinois
Black Hawk College
6600 Thirty-Fourth Avenue
Moline, IL 61265-5899
www.bhc.edu

City Colleges of Chicago, Kennedy-King College
6800 South Wentworth Avenue
Chicago, IL 60621
www.ccc.edu

Indiana
Ivy Tech State College, Central Indiana
1 West Twenty-Sixth Street
Indianapolis, IN 46206-1763
www.ivy.tec.in.us/indianapolis

Ivy Tech State College, Lafayette
3101 South Creasy Lane
P.O. Box 6299
Lafayette, IN 47905-5266
www.laf.ivy.tec.in.us

Iowa
Northwest Iowa Community College
603 West Park Street
Sheldon, IA 51201

Kansas
Flint Hills Technical College
3301 West Eighteenth Street
Emporia, KS 66801

Kaw Area Technical School
5724 Huntoon
Topeka, KS 66604

Kentucky
Ashland Technical College
4818 Roberts Drive
Ashland, KY 41102-9046
www.ashland-rtc.org

Jefferson Technical College
727 West Chestnut Street
Louisville, KY 40203-2036

Louisiana
Delgado Community College
501 City Park Avenue
New Orleans, LA 70119

Louisiana Technical College, Morgan Smith Campus
1230 North Main Street
Jennings, LA 70546

Maine
Central Maine Technical College
1250 Turner Street
Auburn, ME 42106
www.cmtc.net

Northern Maine Technical College
33 Edgemont Drive
Presque Isle, ME 47692
www.nmtc.net

Maryland
Lincoln Technical Institute
9325 Snowden River Parkway
Columbia, MD 21046
www.lincolntech.com

Montgomery College
900 Hungerford Drive
Rockville, MD 20850
www.montgomerycollege.com

Massachusetts
Massachusetts Bay Community College
50 Oakland Street
Wellesley Hills, MA 02481-5399
www.mbcc.mass.edu

Michigan
Ferris State University
901 South State Street
Big Rapids, MI 49307-2251
www.ferris.edu

Henry Ford Community College
5101 Evergreen Road
Dearborn, MI 48128
www.hfcc.net

Minnesota
Northwest Technical College, Bemidji
905 Grant Avenue SE
Bemidji, MN 56601
www.ntc-online.com

Riverland Community College
1900 Eighth Avenue NW
Austin, MN 55912
www.riverland.cc.mn.us

Mississippi
East Mississippi Community College
P.O. Box 158
Scooba, MS 39358-0158
www.emcc.cc.ms.us

Missouri
Jefferson College
1000 Viking Drive
Hillsboro, MO 63050-2440
www.jeffco.edu

Linn State Technical College
One Technology Drive
Linn, MO 65051-9607
www.linnstate.edu

Montana
Montana State University, Billings
College of Technology
3803 Central Avenue
Billings, MT 59102-9856
www.cot.msubillings.edu

Nebraska
Northeast Community College
801 East Benjamin
Norfolk, NE 68702-0469
http://alpha.necc.cc.ne.us

Southeast Community College Area
1111 O Street, Suite 111
Lincoln, NE 68508-3614
www.college.sccm.cc.ne.us

Nevada
Community College of Southern Nevada
3200 East Cheyenne Avenue
Las Vegas, NV 89030

New Jersey
Lincoln Technical Institute
2299 Vauxhall Road
Union, NJ 07083

Pennco Tech
P.O. Box 1427
99 Erial Road
Blackwood, NJ 08012
www.penncotech.com

New Mexico
Albuquerque Technical Vocational Institute
525 Buena Vista SE
Albuquerque, NM 87106
www.tvi.cc.nm.us

New Mexico Junior College
5317 Lovington Highway
Hobbs, NM 88240
www.nmjc.cc.nm.us

New York
Columbia-Greene Community College
4400 Route 23
Hudson, NY 12534

Suffolk County Community College, Ammerman Campus
533 College Road
Selden, NY 11784

North Carolina
Central Piedmont Community College
P.O. Box 35009
Charlotte, NC 28235-5009

Forsyth Technical Community College
2100 Silas Creek Parkway
Winston Salem, NC 27103-5197
www.forsyth.tec.nc.us

North Dakota
Bismarck State College
1500 Edwards Avenue
Bismarck, ND 58501
www.bismarckstate.com

North Dakota State College of Science
800 North Sixth Street
Wahpeton, ND 58076
www.ndscs.nodak.edu

Ohio
Great Oaks Institute of Technology and Career Development
3254 East Kemper Road
Cincinnati, OH 45241

University of Northwestern Ohio
1441 North Cable Road
Lima, OH 45805
www.unoh.edu

Oklahoma
Autry Technology Center
1201 West Willow
Enid, OK 73703-2506

Oklahoma State University, Okmulgee
1801 East Fourth Street
Okmulgee, OK 74447-3901

Oregon
Lane Community College
4000 East Thirtieth Avenue
Eugene, OR 97405
http://Lanecc.edu

Mt. Hood Community College
26000 Southeast Stark Street
Gresham, OR 97030
www.mhcc.cc.or.us

Pennsylvania
Automotive Training Center
114 Pickering Way
Exton, PA 19341-1310
www.autotraining.com

Lincoln Technical Institute
9191 Torresdale Avenue
Philadelphia, PA 19136

Rhode Island
New England Institute of Technology
2500 Post Road
Warwick, RI 02886-2244

South Carolina
Greenville Technical College
506 South Pleasantburg Drive
Greenville, SC 29607
www.greenvilletech.com

Spartanburg Technical College
Business I-85
Spartanburg, SC 29305
www.spt.tec.sc.us

South Dakota
Southeast Technical Institute
2301 Career Place
Sioux Falls, SD 57107-1301
www.sti.tec.sd.us

Western Dakota Technical Institute
800 Mickelson Drive
Rapid City, SD 57703-4018
www.westerndakotatech.org

Tennessee
Tennessee Technology Center, Elizabethton
1500 Arney Street
Elizabethton, TN 37643
http://elizabethton.tec.tn.us

Tennessee Technology Center, Hartsville
716 Mcmurry Boulevard, Highway 25
Hartsville, TN 37074
http://hartsville.tec.tn.us

Texas
Amarillo College
2200 South Washington
Amarillo, TX 79109
www.actx.edu

American Trades Institute
6627 Maple Avenue
Dallas, TX 75235
www.aticareertraining.com

Utah
Bridgerland Applied Technology Center
1301 North 600 W
Logan, UT 84321
www.batc.tec.ut.us

Utah Career College
1902 West 7800 S
West Jordan, UT 84088
www.utahcollege.com

Vermont
Vermont Technical College
P.O. Box 500
Randolph Center, VT 05061-0500

Virginia
Advanced Technology Institute
5700 Southern Boulevard, Suite 100
Virginia Beach, VA 23462
www.aticareers.com

Norfolk Public Schools Skills Center
922 West Twenty-First Street
Norfolk, VA 23517
www.nps.k12.va.us/schools/skillscenter/index.html

Washington
Perry Technical Institute
2011 West Washington Avenue
Yakima, WA 98903-1296
www.perrytech.net

Yakima Valley Community College
Sixteenth and Nob Hill Boulevard
Yakima, WA 98907-2520
www.yvcc.cc.wa.us

West Virginia
Fred W. Eberle Technical Center
Route 5, Box 2
Buckhannon, WV 26201

James Rumsey Technical Institute
Route 6, Box 268
Martinsburg, WV 25401

Wisconsin
Gateway Technical College
3520 Thirtieth Avenue
Kenosha, WI 53144-1690
www.gateway.tec.wi.us

Madison Area Technical College
3550 Anderson Street
Madison, WI 53704
www.madison.tec.wi.us

Wyoming
Casper College
125 College Drive
Casper, WY 82601-4699
www.cc.whecn.edu

Wyoming Technical Institute
4373 North Third
Laramie, WY 82072-9519
www.wyomingtech.com

Puerto Rico
Liceo de Arte y Tecnologia
405 Ponce de Leon Avenue
Box 2346
Hato Rey, PR 00919
www.Liceopr.com

CANADA

The following are a few of the many schools offering automotive technology training in Canada. Also consult the Association of Canadian Community Colleges and schoolfinder.com for more information.

Alberta
Lethbridge Community College
3000 College Drive South
Lethbridge, Alberta T1K 1L6
www.lethbridgec.ab.ca

British Columbia
British Columbia Institute of Technology
3700 Willingdon Avenue
Burnaby, British Columbia V5G 3H2
www.bcit.bc.ca/

Vancouver Community College
City Centre Campus
250 West Pender Street
Vancouver, British Columbia V6B 1S9
www.vcc.bc.ca

Manitoba
Assiniboine Community College
1430 Victoria Avenue East
Brandon, Manitoba R7A 2A9
www.assiniboinec.mb.ca

New Brunswick
New Brunswick Community College, St. John
P.O. Box 2270
Grandview Avenue
Saint John, New Brunswick E2L 3V1
www.saintjohn.nbcc.nb.ca

Newfoundland
College of the North Atlantic
432 Massachusetts Drive
P.O. Box 1693
St. John's, Newfoundland A1C 5P7
www.northatlantic.nf.ca

Ontario

Centennial College of Applied Arts & Technology
P.O. Box 631, Station A, 41 Progress Court
Scarborough, Ontario M1K 5E9
www.cencol.on.ca

Prince Edward Island

Holland College
Royalty Centre
140 Weymouth
Charlottetown, Prince Edward Island C1A 4Z1
www.hollandc.pe.ca

Quebec

ICS Canadian LTD
9001 Avon Road
Montreal, Quebec H4X 2G9
http://ics-canada.com

Saskatchewan

Parkland College
290 Prince William Dr.
Melville, Saskatchewan S0A 2P0
http://mcs.msd.sk.ca/parkland